About the author

David Stone has lived in a small town for most of his life and has had a variety of jobs. Writing books is something he has wanted to do for a while. This is his first book, an adventure that will take you back to your childhood.

THE ADVENTURES OF TOM, JACK AND JOE

David Stone

THE ADVENTURES OF TOM, JACK AND JOE

Vanguard Press

The Wrong Turn

Once upon a time, far, far away, there stood a cottage in the middle of the woods. This cottage was small but beautiful, built from ancient wood and slate. It also had a quirky, thatched roof, which made it look like something out of a fairy tale.

This was the home of three little boys – Tom, Jack and Joe – and they lived in this cottage with their parents, Rosie and George. It was a happy little family, but the three sons didn't spend much time in the cottage: they much preferred roaming the woods and exploring their surroundings, something which their parents encouraged them to do.

Tom was the eldest of the boys, and he always looked after his two younger brothers; he was extremely protective of them both. Jack was the second eldest, and he was the most adventurous of the three; he loved going exploring and finding unusual things. And last but not least, there was little Joe, who was the baby of the three brothers. While he looked up to Tom and Jack a lot, he was always trying to find his feet and become independent, something he hadn't achieved quite yet.

One beautiful sunny morning, the boys woke up and decided to go on an adventure, much to the amusement of their parents – the brothers *always* wanted to go on adventures!

They didn't know what was in store for them, or what was out there waiting for them in the woods, but they were excited to find out.

After eating their breakfast and packing some supplies for their journey ahead, they were off.

The trees in the woods looked very pretty with the sun shining down on them and illuminating their leaves, and the boys decided to head in a direction they very rarely went – they usually avoided it as it was steep and downhill. Still, they were looking for an adventure, and they were bound to find it if they broadened their horizons and went somewhere new.

So, they set off in that direction, talking excitedly as they thought of all the things they could encounter on their adventure. They walked for hours, happy in their little group, and when their stomachs started grumbling, they sat down and ate their lunch, under the cooling shade of a huge tree.

After an hour or so of relaxing, they set off again, walking at first and then running faster and faster as they became even more excited.

The trouble was, they were now running so fast that they couldn't tell where they were going, and before he knew what was happening, Joe had slipped down a steep embankment, falling into some sinking sand at the bottom.

"Help!" he shouted, straining his voice so his brothers could hear him. "I'm stuck in the quicksand!"

Tom and Jack heard their little brother's voice, but it was a good few minutes before they were able to stumble down the steep hill and find out where he was.

Tom saw him first – a little head bobbing up and down in the quicksand – and pointed him out to his brother before rummaging through his rucksack. They'd brought food and drink with them for the journey, but also several pieces of equipment that their parents had insisted they take as well. One of these pieces of equipment was a long, thick rope, and Tom was glad they'd made them bring it – it was about to come in very handy.

"Grab this rope and put it around you!" Tom shouted, throwing it to Joe.

It landed a few feet away from him, but the youngest sibling was just about able to reach out for it and tie it around his waist.

"Now we're going to pull you out!"

"OK!" replied Joe, who sounded extremely scared at the thought.

Tom and Jack then pulled on the rope with all their might, their feet digging into the soil beneath them as they dealt with the weight of their little brother.

Finally, Joe emerged at the side of the quicksand, completely drained of energy and panting for air.

"I thought you were a gonna, bro!" said Tom, who was also trying to catch his breath.

"Me too," agreed Jack, whose face was bright red from the exertion.

"Nah, not a chance," said Joe, laughing. "You've got to put up with me a little bit longer. You don't get rid of me that easily!"

"Pity," Tom said, laughing.

All three of them were completely exhausted from the ordeal, so they all lay down on the bank to have a rest.

After a while, Tom looked up at the sky, which could just about be seen through the leaves of the trees. "It'll be getting dark soon."

"We'll have to find somewhere to camp," replied Jack.

"Come on then," said Tom, as he got to his feet and had a big stretch. "We'll carry on and when we find a decent spot, we'll put up the tent."

He then pulled his two brothers to their feet and they all set off together, making sure to keep clear of the boggy quicksand.

After a few miles of walking, the three siblings came to a large clearing in the woods.

"This looks like a good place to set up camp," said Joe, excited at the prospect of putting the tent up with his brothers. He'd never been able to do it on his own, and he always loved watching Tom and Jack work together – he always learned so much.

"Perfect," Tom replied. "You two start unpacking and I'll go and get some wood to make a fire."

"Don't go too far!" shouted Joe, looking at the darkening sky. He didn't like the darkness, and he wanted to make sure Tom would be back before it got too dark to see.

"I won't," replied his brother, before setting off on his wood-finding mission. Tom had been in the scouts, and he knew everything there was to know about building and lighting a fire, from what kind of wood to pick, to how to get that first flame to set the wood alight.

Joe and Jack started unpacking their rucksacks, putting their food and drink in a pile so they could see how much they had, then getting the tent out of its bag so they could set it up.

They'd been hoping Tom would be back in time to help them with the tent, but it was now starting to get really dark, so they thought they'd do it themselves while there was still a little bit of daylight left. To make matters worse, a thick mist had now started to come down, settling all around the clearing.

"I'm getting cold," said Joe, as they finished sorting the tent out. He went over to his bag and put another jumper on, then handed a scarf to his brother.

Just as Jack was reaching out to take the scarf, he whispered, "Shh! Did you hear that?"

"Hear what?" asked Joe, as he strained his ears to listen.

"An owl," whispered Jack. "There in the tree!"

"Oh yeah, I can see him!" said Joe excitedly. He'd never seen an owl up close before, and he wished they'd brought some binoculars with them so they could have an even closer look.

It went quiet then for a few minutes, and just as Joe and Jack were about to go and sit in the tent to wait for their brother, a loud sound echoed around the clearing – the sound of a twig breaking on the forest floor.

"Who's there?" asked Jack, as his little brother hid behind him, scared.

There was no response – there was seemingly nobody there.

But then there was another sound, a kind of rustling that was coming from the bushes next to the tent.

Slowly, the two brothers walked over to it, bending down and squinting at the leaves in the darkness.

The next sound they heard sent shivers down their spines: it was a growl, low and quiet, coming from the bush. This was accompanied by a flash of a pair of eyes, staring out from the leaves and looking directly at the boys.

"What is it?" asked Joe, completely terrified.

"I think…" replied Jack quietly, his voice low, "I think it's a wolf."

It was a wolf all right, and as it emerged from out of the bushes and started creeping towards them, it breathed heavily and licked its lips. He was obviously looking for his next meal.

The two boys were backing away slowly, but after a few seconds, Jack turned to his brother and whispered, "When I say run, I want you to run, and don't look back."

"But what about you?" asked Joe, mortified at the idea. "I can't leave you here to defend yourself!"

"Go, *now*!" said Jack, his only thought being to keep his little brother safe.

Just at that moment, however, Tom appeared as if from nowhere, dropping the firewood on the ground and scaring away the wolf, who disappeared into the night at the loud sound.

"That was close!" he said. "Are you guys both OK?"

"Yeah, fine," said Jack, as he tried to get his pulse to return to normal – his heart had been hammering in his chest at the sight of the wolf.

Joe, however, wasn't fine; he'd been so frightened that he'd wet himself, and had then passed out on the floor.

"Joe, Joe! Are you all right?" asked Jack, concerned.

Tom leaned down over Joe to check he was breathing. "He's fine," he told his brother. "Just let him sleep it off, and by the time he wakes up, we'll have some food ready for him. That'll make him feel better."

"Well, we'd better make the fire first if we're to cook the food," said Jack, staring at the pile of wood Tom had dropped. "Is that enough?"

"It should be," said Tom. "I'll get going on it now."

"You were gone for ages," said Jack. "Were you OK?"

"I just got a bit lost in the woods," Tom explained. "I took the wrong turn and was going in the wrong direction for a while. It's a good job I realised my mistake when I did, or who knows what could have happened with that wolf?"

Jack nodded. "We'll have to keep a look out tonight in case it comes back – we'll sleep in shifts."

"Right," said Tom, as he set about getting the fire sorted.

Soon, there was a small but effective fire going in the middle of the clearing, the light and the warmth waking Joe up from his sleep.

The first thing he said as he came round was, "Mmm, I'm starving!" which made his brothers laugh, and as Tom started cooking the food, the two of them kept pulling Joe's leg and making jokes.

"Maybe Joe shouldn't take a turn as lookout – he might faint again!"

Joe ignored them as he changed his trousers and came to sit by the fire. "What's for tea?"

"There you go, brother," said Tom, as he dished up the food. "Beans, bacon and eggs. That'll fill you up, and make you feel much better."

"Thanks," Joe replied, as he tucked into his food.

Soon, all was silent while the brothers ate.

By the time they were full, all three of them were yawning loudly, but Tom agreed to stay up to be first on watch should the wolf come back.

Joe and Jack went in the tent and got into their sleeping bags, while Tom sat at the tent entrance, zipped up in his own sleeping bag.

He peered out at the forest around them. All was still.

*****

The next day came around, and by the time the sun was up and shining, the three brothers had had a hearty breakfast of bread and jam. Then, it was time for them to pack up and continue on their adventure.

After walking for several miles, Joe shouted out, "I see a stream! I'll get some water."

The three of them ran over to the stream, filling up their bottles and having a quick wash in the refreshing water.

"I wonder where we are," said Jack. He didn't recognise this stream – or any of their surroundings – at all.

"We seem to be lost," said Tom. "Perhaps we took a wrong turn somewhere."

Tom glanced around and spotted a man a little further down the stream, washing his hands in the water. "Maybe he can tell us where we are, and how far we are from home."

"Yes, he looks like he might be a farmer, so there could be a farm nearby," said Jack, as they walked over to the man.

"Hello!" shouted Tom.

"Hello there, can I help you?" asked the farmer.

"We were just wondering where we were – what is this place called?"

"Oh I see," he replied. "It's called Meadows, and there's a farm down there called Meadows Farm." He pointed to his left. "It's quite easy to find, and if you're looking for food, you might be able to get some eggs and milk from there."

"Oh, thank you, sir," said Joe. "We'll be on our way then."

With that, the three brothers set off in the direction of the farm, and when they got to the gates, they saw a middle-aged woman standing in one of the fields, feeding a brood of hens.

"Hello, can I help you, children?" asked the farmer's wife.

"We were wondering if we could buy some eggs and milk from you," said Tom. "A farmer pointed this place out to us."

"Of course!" she replied, smiling kindly. "Just follow me around to the farm."

She walked off in the direction of a large farmhouse, and they followed behind her, happy to be able to get some more food – their own supplies were dwindling.

"There you go," she said, as she handed them a bundle wrapped in newspaper. "There's some milk, bread, butter and eggs."

"Thank you," replied Jack, giving her some money. "Do you happen to have a map of the area by any chance?"

"Good thinking," said Joe, as the farmer's wife went off to have a look, and soon she'd returned with an old, crinkled map of the farm and its surrounding land.

"You can keep this," she said. "Now, if you'll excuse me, I must get back to my chickens."

"Right," said Tom, getting down to business. "Let's look at this map of Meadows Farm."

Jack and Joe moved closer to their brother, all of them peering at the crumpled map in his hands.

"We need to follow the road around, cross the river, go down the hill and then head back into the woods. We should be home sometime tomorrow," said Tom.

"Great!" said Jack. "Come on, you two, let's go!"

So they set off again, happy in the knowledge that they knew where they were going, and that they had more food and drink for when they next had to set up camp.

Unfortunately, their way back home was about to prove as problematic as their first day – but this time, it wasn't a wolf who stepped into their path, but a bull.

"A bull!" shouted Jack. "Run!"

All three of the brothers ran as fast as they could, although their heavy rucksacks slowed them down.

"He's catching up to me!" screamed Joe, his voice full of panic.

"You have to take your red jumper off!" shouted Jack. "Bulls are attracted to red!"

"OK," replied Joe, as he ran and jumped over the fence, landing straight in a huge pile of mud.

His brothers were standing next to him, laughing their socks off. They'd climbed over the fence instead of jumped, and had consequently landed upright, instead of on their backs in a mud pile.

"Come on, Joe, let's get you cleaned up," Tom said, still laughing.

They found the stream they'd used earlier and Joe washed himself as much as he could.

"That's better," he said, as he now felt fresh, although there were still bits of dirt here and there. "Come on, you two," he added, "we need to find the big river next."

Glancing at the map again, the three brothers set off once more, finally coming to the river a couple of hours later.

There was just one problem.

"Oh no, there's no bridge to cross," said Joe.

"Hang on a minute," said Tom. "I need to think... OK, what if we get some rope and put it around that tree over there? Then we can swing across to the other side of the river."

"OK," said Jack, not sounding entirely convinced. He watched as his older brother tied the rope around the tree.

"Here goes, Joe. You go first because you're the lightest," suggested Tom.

"OK, here I come!" shouted Joe, as he grabbed the rope and swung across the rushing river, landing on the bank on the other side. "I made it! Now it's your turn, Jack."

"Ready!" he replied, but as Jack swung across, they heard the branch crack. Still, Jack got across safely, joining Joe on the opposite river bank as he sent the rope back to Tom.

So far, so good.

When the eldest brother swung across, however, the branch gave way completely and he fell into the river, where the current swept him away. It was so fast that he was gone in an instant.

The two brothers ran to the side of the river to see if they could locate Tom, but as the water was rushing by so quickly, it was incredibly hard to see anything.

Still, they kept on looking for him, and after a few minutes they noticed something lying against a rock, in a part of the river where the current wasn't quite so strong.

As they got near to it, they could see that it was Tom, lying there and looking like he'd broken his leg and his arm. He also had a large bruise on his head.

The two brothers scrambled over to Tom, being careful as they moved him. He was unconscious but breathing, but most of all, he was cold. Very cold.

"I'll make a fire to keep him warm," said Jack.

"No, I'll just wrap him up in some more clothes; we have to go and get help!" shouted Joe.

"You're right. You stay here while I go and find someone, OK?"

Joe agreed and Jack replied, "I'll be back soon."

With that, Jack headed off back the way they'd come, in the direction of the farm.

He was gone for a very long time.

*****

Half an hour later, before he'd got anywhere near the farm, Jack came to a house on the hill.

He knocked on the door and waited, and it was soon opened by a lady who asked, "Can I help you?"

"I'm looking for a doctor," Jack replied. "It's urgent."

"My husband's a doctor, and I'm a nurse," she replied. "What's wrong?"

Jack told the woman what had happened, as quickly as he could, and when he was finished she said, "I'll just get my bag."

The woman introduced Jack to her husband and then the three of them set off for the river. Unfortunately, they took a wrong turn on the way, and it was a while before they found Joe and Tom.

Tom was still unconscious, so they had to make a stretcher to carry him back to the house, and when they got there, the doctor and the nurse laid him out on the bed in the spare room.

"Here we are, back home," said the doctor, as he turned to face Jack and Joe. "He'll need a lot of bed rest, but he can stay here with us until he's recovered – who better to look after him than a doctor and a nurse? You'd better go and tell your parents what's happened; he could be here for several weeks."

So, Jack and Joe went home, but they made sure to visit their brother whenever they could.

The weeks went by and the two brothers prayed for Tom's recovery, hoping he would get better soon.

By the sixth week when they went to visit him, Tom was starting to come round, and as he opened his eyes and smiled, he asked, "Where am I?"

"You've had a fall, and you're staying at a doctor's house," Jack told him.

Just then, the doctor came in. "How's my patient this morning?" he asked.

"Just a bit confused," said Tom.

"I'm not surprised," he replied. "You've had a bit of a fall in the water – you've been in the wars."

"I've got a pain in my leg and my arm," Tom said.

"Yes, you've broken them," said the doctor. "But don't worry, they'll soon be healed enough so you can go home."

And within two weeks, that is exactly what they did.

Their parents were waiting for them on the doorstep of the cottage, and when they saw Tom, they ran up to him and hugged him tightly.

Once they were all inside and sitting down to dinner, Joe turned to Tom and said, "You know what? You really are a pain in the neck!"

"Or a pain in the leg," suggested Tom, as they all began to laugh.

"One's thing for sure – I'll never take the wrong turn again!"

The Indian and the Animals

Tom, Jack and Joe loved going on adventures, and once again, they were preparing to leave their little cottage in the woods and head out into the big world beyond. What would they get up to this time? Hold on for the ride of your life!

The brothers were very excited about going on another adventure, especially as it was summer and their parents had let them hire horses for the week. They'd all taken riding lessons the summer before, and as they left the cottage and set out, the three of them felt like cowboys in an old Western film.

The weather was amazing; the sun was shining, the birds were singing, and it was warm enough for them to go off on their adventure without needing coats or even jackets. It was going to be a good trip.

They were riding down the road on their horses, laughing and joking with each other. Tom, as the eldest, was keeping track of where they were going so they didn't get lost (this usually happened to them quite a lot), whereas Jack (the middle child) and Joe (the youngest) were only concerned with having fun.

"The sun is bright, the sky is blue, the clouds are white, and so are both of you," Joe sang, trying to impress his brothers. He liked coming up with little rhymes, and he loved it when he could make his brothers laugh.

Both of them chuckled at their little brother as they continued to climb up into the mountains. It was gorgeous up there, with the sun glinting off the mountain peaks. There wasn't a single cloud in sight.

Jack shouted, "It's very picturesque here!"

"It is," agreed Joe. "And you can hear your voice echo in the mountains!" He waited for the sound of his words to bounce back to him, smiling when the echo reached his ears. Echoes always fascinated him.

"Look down there," said Tom, as he pointed his finger at a camp located in one of the valleys. There was a thin layer of mist hanging over the top, making the whole place seem like something out of a fairy tale.

"It looks like an Indian camp," said Jack, taking in the wigwams and the smoke rising from several fires that were dotted around the valley.

"Come on, let's go and explore it!" shouted Joe, full of excitement at the prospect. He'd never been in an Indian camp before.

His brothers agreed with him, and soon the three of them were in the valley, riding up to one of the wigwams at the edge of the camp. The whole place smelled like wood smoke, and many people were bustling about, fetching wood and water and maintaining the wigwams in which they slept.

A young Indian boy – who looked to be a similar age to the brothers – walked out of the wigwam and went over to Tom, Jack and Joe.

"How," he said, smiling. "My name is Cumbow. What brings you here?"

"We're going on a camping holiday around these parts," said Tom. "We saw your camp and couldn't help but come and have a look. It's nice to meet you."

Jack added, "I'm Jack, and these are my brothers, Tom and Joe."

Everyone said hello, and just as they were finishing their greetings, an older man walked over to the group.

"This is my grandfather, Takey," said Cumbow, smiling up at him.

"Hello," he replied.

"Nice to meet you," the brothers said.

Cumbow told his grandfather about the brothers' camping trip.

"You have to be careful around here," Takey warned. "There are bears, snakes, crocodiles, bats... all kinds of dangerous and scary creatures." He then put his hands into a praying position and added, "Peace be with you," before walking off and entering one of the wigwams.

"Let me show you around," said Cumbow, as he took them on a tour of the camp. Wherever they went, Indian children and adults said hello, all of them interested in the boys and what they were doing in the area. More people warned them of the dangerous animals, giving them advice which the brothers gratefully accepted.

After a while, they headed out of the camp, walking in the sun with their new friend, Cumbow. They'd left their horses with the Indians, in order to give them a bit of a rest. After all, they'd been travelling for several hours in the heat.

Cumbow showed them many different places where he went to fish in the lake, as well as how he fished using his harpoon, and after quite a while spent walking, all four of the boys were hot and tired.

The lake looked so inviting – with the sun glinting off the bright blue surface – that it gave Joe an idea. "I'm going to have a swim," he informed the others, before getting changed and jumping into the water. "Come on, you guys, it's nice and warm!" he shouted.

Tom and Jack thought this was a great idea, and with no hesitation whatsoever, they both changed and jumped into the lake after their brother, splashing Joe as they landed in the warm, soothing water.

Cumbow – who had bathed in the water already that morning – sat on the bank, watching the brothers as they splashed each other, laughing heartily.

Jack then swum over to Tom, whispering, "Come on, let's get Joe – we'll put his head under the water for a laugh!" They were always playing pranks on their little brother, as he was the youngest, but Joe never seemed to mind – in fact, he seemed to enjoy messing around with his brothers.

Just then, Cumbow stood up on the bank and shouted out, "Crocodiles!"

The three boys froze. They'd been having so much fun in the water that they hadn't seen the crocodiles approach them, and now two crocs were staring at the three of them with their black, beady eyes.

"Come on!" shouted Cumbow, breaking them out of their trance, and the three brothers swam to the bank as fast as they could, scrambling out of the water just in the nick of time.

The crocodiles snapped at their heels, their long, pointed teeth bared for all to see.

Joe shuddered. That had been a close call, far too close.

"You lot OK?" Cumbow asked, concerned for his new friends.

"Yes," replied Jack and Tom in unison.

They looked a little shaken up but were otherwise fine, while Joe looked as white as a sheet. It was as if he'd just seen a ghost. He took a few deep breaths in an attempt to stop himself from fainting, then joined the others as they began to walk away from the lake. They'd had enough of the water for one day.

So, the three brothers continued to travel on their journey with Cumbow, and soon the sky began to darken as the sun started its descent to the horizon.

Joe stared at the sunset. "Oh, it's beautiful," he remarked. He'd never seen a sunset so stunning before, and neither had Jack or Tom.

"It certainly is," said Cumbow. "I enjoy the sunset every night. And the sunrise every morning is just as beautiful."

"Well, it'll be dark soon," said Tom, looking at the horizon. "We'd better set up camp now. Cumbow, will you stay with us tonight?"

Their new friend nodded. He enjoyed their company, and it was far too late to be walking back to the camp now. He'd told his grandfather before he left that he may stay with Tom, Jack and Joe overnight, so he knew he wouldn't be worried.

With that, the three brothers opened their rucksacks and bags and took out their tent. Cumbow – who was used to wigwams but not camping tents – watched in awe as they put it up; they'd had so much practice with the tent that they got it up in no time at all, and Cumbow was impressed.

The four friends then ate some food the brothers had brought with them, before lying down beneath the stars. The twinkling lights in the sky were just as beautiful as the sunset had been, although in a different way.

"It's quiet around here," said Tom.

Cumbow, however, disagreed. "On the contrary, it's never quiet here. If you close your eyes, you will hear all sorts of animals around you."

Intrigued, the three brothers did as Cumbow suggested, closing their eyes and focusing on the sounds they could hear.

Joe heard a sniffing kind of noise, like an animal snuffling in the undergrowth, while Tom could hear the distant flapping of a bird's wings. Jack could hear the far cry of an animal calling out, and then after a few seconds, the returning cry of its mate.

Cumbow was right: the country was crawling with animals, all of them coming together to make a wild cacophony of sounds, you just had to make the effort to listen to them.

"Well, it's going to be a long day tomorrow," said Tom finally.

"Yes," said Jack. "We should get some rest."

Soon, all four of them had fallen asleep, while the sounds of the mountain carried on all around them.

*****

When morning came, Cumbow was the first up, and leaving the brothers to sleep in a little more, he went out to find something to have for breakfast.

The sun was slowly starting to heat the ground as he made his way to the lake and, checking for crocodiles first, he speared a few fish with his harpoon.

He also gathered some wood, and once he was back at the camp, he started a little fire. It was the smell of the fish cooking on the fire that woke up the three brothers.

"That smells amazing," said Tom, as he slowly sat up and rubbed at his eyes.

"Did you catch that?" asked Jack.

Cumbow nodded. "Freshly caught this morning. Now eat it while it's still warm."

The four friends ate the fish, washing it down with the juice they'd brought with them in their rucksacks. The fish tasted lovely, and they all thanked Cumbow for going and getting it for them.

They were soon all full, and after packing up their tent and the rest of their camp, it was time to move on.

"Come," said Cumbow, as he led them into the forest.

It was cooler there – under the shade of the trees – and the brothers walked a little slower, making the most of the pleasant temperature.

There were even more animal noises around here, and intrigued about a certain sound he could hear, Tom took out a pair of binoculars from his bag.

He often forgot to bring the binoculars along on their adventures, but he was glad he'd brought them this time, as he soon spotted a large eagle, flying around above them. It was a majestic sight: he was soaring around in the bright blue sky, as if he owned the very air up there.

Tom pointed the beautiful bird out to his brothers and Cumbow, and soon all four of them were pointing at the eagle and laughing in delight.

Unfortunately, they were so caught up with staring at the bird that they didn't notice a huge, black bear coming towards them, and it wasn't until the bear – who was now quite close to the group – started making loud 'roar' noises that they noticed him at all.

"Run!" shouted Tom to the others, almost dropping his binoculars in his effort to run away.

"Oh my God, that's a big bear!" said Joe, as he ran after his brother, tripping over a branch on the ground as he went. If he thought the crocodile from the day before was scary, it was nothing compared to the sight of a large, adult bear, standing on its hind legs and towering over them as it roared madly.

Joe started shivering as he tried to get to his feet again.

"Get up, quick!" said Jack. "You haven't time to sit down!" He then grabbed his little brother, giving him a piggy back ride to safety.

The three brothers stopped, all of them panting with exhaustion and looking wildly around them in case the bear was still in the vicinity.

Just then, Cumbow joined them, also looking a little out of breath. "Don't worry, I scared the bear off with this." He held up the harpoon he'd used to catch that morning's breakfast. "He ran off into the trees."

"Thank you, Cumbow," said Joe, who thought that he actually might faint. His heart was beating faster than it ever had before.

"That was close," said Tom. "Yes, thanks, Cumbow."

Jack agreed, and Cumbow shrugged. "It was nothing."

Joe was still staring at the trees where he'd last seen the bear, his mouth hanging wide open like he was trying to catch flies. He hoped he'd never see a bear in the wild ever again.

"Let's go," said Tom. "I don't think we should stick around here – it could come back."

The others agreed, and soon they were on their way yet again.

"What a day this has been!" said Jack, as the four of them carried on through the forest.

"It's certainly been interesting," agreed Tom, as they walked under tree branches and over roots.

They still had a long way to go, and the sight of the bear had rattled them: what else would they come across? Cumbow's grandfather (as well as many others at the Indian camp) had warned them about such dangerous animals, but they didn't think they'd encounter quite so many of them in such a short amount of time. What would be next?

Not knowing what else was out there, the brothers and Cumbow stuck as close together as possible, and after another hour or two of walking, the decision was made to have a rest for a while.

Their rest, however, wasn't very restful, as when Jack sat down on the forest floor, a snake immediately crawled up his trouser leg, causing him to freeze in fear. "Snake!" he shouted, not able to say anything else. "Snake!"

The others all stood back from him, but as the snake crawled out of his trouser leg again, another one slithered up to Tom and bit him on the ankle before he'd even seen it.

"Ouch! What was that?"

Cumbow frowned as he watched both of the snakes slither away. "This is serious; I have to get you back to the camp. My grandfather will know what to do."

"Can you walk?" asked Joe.

Tom tried to put one foot in front of the other, and when he nearly fell over, his brothers moved over to catch him.

"We'll get you back to the camp," said Joe, putting his arm around Tom as Jack did the same on his other side.

The three brothers continued to walk like this through the forest, while Cumbow led the way and looked out for any other dangerous animals that may cross their path.

Eventually – after what felt like forever – they found their way back to the Indian camp, and Cumbow immediately ran off to find Takey.

"Grandfather!" he shouted. "Come and help! My friend has been bitten by a snake!"

By now, Tom was beginning to burn up, his face as red as the glowing sun of the sunset the night before.

Takey, however, was calm and collected, and he even sang an old Indian song to himself as he put Tom inside one of the wigwams and bathed his head with a sponge. He then extracted the poison from Tom's leg, spitting it out onto the floor before wiping his mouth.

"There you go," he said, as he continued to hum the little tune.

Joe and Jack sat by Tom's bedside, while Cumbow fetched water for them all to drink.

"Is the poison gone?" asked Jack, to which Takey nodded.

"It is gone, though it will be a bit of a waiting game for him now. Only time will tell what will happen." He glanced at Tom, who had gone to sleep. "I'll leave him to rest," added Takey, before leaving the four boys alone in the wigwam.

"Do you think he'll be all right?" Joe asked Cumbow, his brow furrowed.

The Indian boy patted Joe's shoulder – he could tell how worried he was about his brother. "My grandfather will talk to the spirits and give Tom something for the pain," he replied. "He's in good hands."

"How long will he have to stay here for?" asked Jack.

"A few days at least," replied Cumbow. "Maybe even weeks. It's hard to say at the moment, but we'll look after him for as long as necessary."

So, a couple of weeks went by, and Tom was starting to feel like his normal self – at least, he'd started teasing

Joe again, so he must have been feeling better. Jack and Joe had made the trip back to their cottage, to tell their parents of what had happened to Tom, before riding back to the camp to be with their brother while he recovered.

Soon, Tom found he was well enough to get up, and the three boys started preparations to leave the camp and go home to their little cottage. Their parents would be waiting for them, and they couldn't wait to get back to their own beds.

As they were leaving, Tom took their little Indian friend aside. "Cumbow, I would like to thank you and your grandfather for helping me."

"We were happy to help," said Cumbow. "Just make sure you're careful on the way home. You always need to keep a lookout for any dangerous animals."

Joe nodded enthusiastically. He never wanted to see a bear, a snake, or a crocodile ever again, and from now on, he and his brothers would be extra careful when they went on their adventures.

Tom, Jack and Joe then said goodbye to Cumbow, Takey and everyone else at the camp, before getting on their horses and heading back home.

They got back to their cottage to find that their parents had made a delicious meal for the three of them, and they had great fun eating every single bit of it.

"What an adventure!" said Jack.

"It was definitely one I'll never forget," agreed Joe.

Tom laughed. "Me neither. Although I think I'd rather *like* to forget the snake part of it!"

The three brothers laughed, thinking of their new friend, Cumbow. One day they'd go back and visit him again, although they hoped that adventure wouldn't be quite as eventful as this one had been!

The Eye of the Storm

And now we tune into another adventure featuring Tom, Jack and Joe – three brothers who love to go on explorations, and who often find themselves in slightly sticky situations.

This time, the brothers had decided to go on a cross-country run, in order to get some exercise and to see some of the surrounding countryside. Their parents had agreed that it would be a good activity for them to do, and they'd set off first thing in the morning.

After a couple of hours, the brothers stopped to catch their breath and to have a drink of water from their bottles.

Jack glanced around them before turning to his brothers. "All these fields look alike."

Tom looked out over the meadow they were in and realised Jack was right: each field looked identical to the next, and with no large landmarks to navigate by, they could be anywhere. "I think we're lost."

Joe groaned. "Again?" It wasn't the first time the three brothers had found themselves in a strange place.

Luckily, the boys had brought some orienteering equipment with them, but unluckily, they couldn't agree on where they needed to go next.

Jack peered at the compass and said, "I think it's this way," pointing straight ahead at the rest of the meadow.

Joe, however, was shaking his head. "No, we need to go over there." He pointed at a stile in the fence, which would take them into the next field.

"You're both wrong; it's down here," Tom replied, looking at the map.

"Oh yeah," said Jack, changing his mind. "The compass says we're facing northeast, so we need to head down there towards those trees."

"Are you sure?" asked Joe, frowning at the map and moving the compass around, as if it would somehow change its mind about where north was. "I wish we could ask someone. There's never anybody around when you need them!"

Tom rolled his eyes. "You're always such a drama queen, Joe. We'll be fine, come on."

Jack laughed as he started walking behind Tom, while Joe brought up the rear, a little embarrassed at being called a drama queen by his older brother.

They continued to run for a few minutes, and as they were going, the temperature started to drop rapidly. It had been nice and sunny that morning, but now the sun had gone behind a huge, grey cloud.

"I'm getting cold," said Jack.

"I know what you mean," replied Joe, shuddering slightly. They were only wearing shorts and T-shirts.

As they continued to run into the next field, they suddenly saw a postman coming towards them along one of the paths. His postbag was empty, so he was obviously on his way home after delivering all of the letters.

"Good day to you," he said.

"Hello," said Tom, as he came to a stop in front of the postman. "Could you please tell us where we are?"

The postman peered over at their map, then after a few seconds of thinking, he pointed to a place on the paper. "I'd say about here. The gypsy camp is just down there," he nodded in the direction of the camp, "so if you get there, you can get to the main road."

"Thank you," said Tom, as the postman went on his way. He then turned to his brothers. "Shall we go to the gypsy camp, then? At least then we'll know where we are."

"Yes!" replied Joe immediately. He'd never seen gypsies before, and he was very interested in meeting some and seeing where they lived.

"OK," said Tom. "Let's go!"

With that, the three boys walked off in the direction the postman had told them, and soon they found themselves at the edge of a large camp – caravans and tents seemed to be the main dwellings, but there was also a lot of outside, communal furniture as well.

"Hello," said Jack, to a man who was passing by. "We got lost and were told your camp is near the road."

"That's right," said the man. "I'm ZingGo."

"These are my two brothers, Jack and Joe, and my name's Tom," said the eldest of the three. "How do you do?"

"What are you doing around here?" asked ZingGo, looking at the running gear they were wearing.

"We're on a cross-country run," said Tom. "It keeps us fit!"

"Tell me about it! I've got the stitch," said Jack, bending over to catch his breath.

Joe said nothing; he just glanced around at the camp, his eyes open wide. There were so many people milling about, and so much to see that he had a hard time keeping up with everything.

"Would you like something to eat?" asked ZingGo, gesturing at a nearby caravan. "This is my home."

"Oh, that would be great," said Joe, finally finding his voice. Joe was always thinking about food, and he never turned down a free meal.

ZingGo nodded as he opened the door to his caravan and called for his family to join them. "This is my brother, Faffos, my wife, Zantear, and my daughter, Zanfaya."

"Hello," said the three brothers, smiling at ZingGo's family.

ZingGo went and stood next to Zanfaya, whispering into her ear before telling the boys, "My daughter will do a dance for you. She is very good."

The brothers sat down on some garden furniture outside the caravan, and while Zanfaya entertained them with her dancing, ZingGo lit a barbeque and started to grill some meat.

Soon, they were all tucking into big, juicy burgers, while ZingGo and his family told them about life as gypsies. They were a tight-knit community, and they even had their own doctor and nurse, should they need any medical treatment. They often took turns cooking and cleaning, and everyone generally helped each other out as much as they could. The boys thought it sounded wonderful.

Before long, the sun was setting, and ZingGo looked out to the horizon. "It will be dark soon. You are welcome to stay tonight if you wish."

"Thank you," said the three brothers, as ZingGo led them into the surprisingly spacious caravan.

"You can sleep here," he said, going over to the seating area and pulling out the sofas, which turned into beds. He then disappeared through a curtain, going to his own sleeping quarters. Zanfaya had gone to stay in her friend's caravan.

The boys lay down on the beds, pulling the blankets over them and settling in for the night.

Not long after they'd fallen asleep, the heavens opened and the rain came pouring down, making a loud pounding noise on the roof of the caravan as the rain drops bounced off it.

It was so loud it woke up Joe, who peered around him in the darkness, scared. "Are you there?" he whispered to

Tom, but Tom was out for the count. "Are you there, Jack?" he whispered again, trying his other brother.

"What is it?" he said.

"Can you hear the rain?" Joe asked.

"Yes, now go back to sleep," Jack replied irritably.

Joe didn't find this quite so easy to do, however, and it was a good couple of hours before he drifted off again, the sound of the rain still lingering in his ears.

*****

Soon, morning came around, and it was ever so cloudy as Joe peered out of the caravan window.

"It doesn't look like it's going to be a very nice day," he said.

Jack and Tom also looked out the window at the gloomy sky, nodding in agreement.

"Morning!" said ZingGo, as he popped his head around the corner. "Did you sleep well?"

"Yes," said Tom, smiling.

"I didn't," said Jack, as he stared at Joe with a frown on his face. "For some reason I kept waking up."

"I'm sorry," said Joe, as he looked down at the floor. He felt bad about waking his brother up, but he didn't like the sound of the rain, and he'd been frightened in the darkness of the caravan.

Just then, a voice came from around the corner, from the caravan's kitchen area. "Who's ready for a fry up, then?" It was Zantear.

"Yes, please!" said the brothers in unison, as they all rubbed their tummies.

ZingGo opened the door of the caravan, setting up the awning before he called for the boys to come out.

"This will fill you up," said Zantear, as she came over and handed them each a big plate loaded with food.

"It smells so good," said Tom, tucking into his eggs.

"It's delicious," agreed Joe, happy now that he had some food inside him.

"Well, that's filled a gap. I could do with a walk now," said Jack, as he stretched his arms and legs.

The boys agreed it was time to go, and ZingGo pointed out the direction to the road.

"Well, thank you for everything," said Jack, as the three brothers headed out of the camp.

ZingGo and his family waved them off, standing under the awning of their caravan and smiling.

"It definitely looks like it's going to rain," said Joe, as they found the main road and walked along it.

He was right: not long after they'd gone into the next field, the clouds got darker and the rain began to pour – harder than it had fallen during the night. Soon, the wind picked up and the rain turned to hail stones, hitting the boys hard on their arms and the tops of their heads.

"We have to find somewhere to shelter!" shouted Tom, in his usual bossy tone of voice. Being the eldest, he was always the one to take charge in these kinds of situations.

It was now extremely cold, and the boys shivered as they walked quickly across the field, their teeth chattering together the whole time.

Then the lightning came, crashing down and striking a nearby tree with such strength that it split down the middle, causing a branch to fall to the ground. The flash of the lightning was so bright that the brothers couldn't look directly at it, and a few seconds later, they all heard the low rumbling sound of the thunder.

"Look!" shouted Tom, pointing at a nearby shed at the edge of the field. "If we run for it, we might make it! Come on!"

"OK!" yelled Jack and Joe, as they all ran to safety of the shed.

Opening the door, they flung themselves in, out of the wind and the hail. The shed was empty apart from some logs and some old fishing gear.

"At least we'll be dry in here for a while," said Tom.

"Now we can do a sing-song together to pass the time," said Joe. "Come on!"

"OK," said Jack and Tom, smiling at Joe's enthusiasm. They had a feeling he wanted to sing to take his mind off the raging storm outside, so they agreed, and soon they were all singing songs they'd learnt while camping with their parents.

As they were singing, Tom started to feel a tingling sensation in his hair, and as he put his hand up to his head, he realised what it was. "Ahh!"

"What is it?" asked Joe.

"It's a spider!" yelled Tom.

"Let's have a look then," said Jack, peering at Tom's hair. "It's a money spider! You're not scared of little money spiders, are you?" He found the idea of his strong, brave big brother being terrified of spiders actually quite amusing.

Joe picked it out of Tom's hair and waved it in front of his face. "It's just a tiny spider!"

"Stop it!" shouted Tom. "Get it away from me!"

"OK, I'm sorry," replied Joe. He did feel a little bad about teasing his older brother, but he was secretly rather happy about getting his own back, because Tom was always teasing him about one thing or another.

Finally, the rain stopped and Tom opened the door to find the sun shining and the birds singing. Rabbits were running around on the grass and butterflies were fluttering past. All was peaceful.

"Come on," he said, "the storm's over. And look, we're next to the river!"

All three of the boys emerged into the sunlight, surprised to see a river right next to them. They'd been so focused on getting into the shed during the storm that they hadn't even noticed it was there.

"I suppose that explains the fishing equipment in the shed," said Tom. "Although it did look very old and rusted. I wish it was new, then we could have gone fishing ourselves."

"Hmm." After thinking for a few seconds, Jack went back into the shed, coming out a few moments later with three long sticks, the ends of which had been filed into points. "We can't use the fishing rods, but we can use these. Remember when Cumbow showed us how to fish using his harpoon?"

Joe nodded enthusiastically. They'd had a great time with Cumbow, the Indian, a few months ago, and if they tried really hard, he thought they'd be able to catch quite a few fish.

So, Jack handed out the sticks and they made their way down the bank and into the river. The water was a little cold on their legs, but the sun shining on their faces more than made up for it, and soon they were happily trying to catch fish with their makeshift harpoons, laughing and having fun the whole time.

They were all glad that the storm was over.

A few minutes later, Joe was just celebrating catching his first fish when he felt raindrops falling on his arms. Looking up at the sky, he saw that a large, black cloud was hovering directly over the river.

"Jack, Tom…? I think the storm might be coming back."

His brothers, however, were so preoccupied with trying to catch a fish that they didn't even hear what their little brother was saying.

Joe was suddenly very cold, his arms coming out in goose bumps and his legs feeling like ice under the water.

"Jack, Tom!"

"What?" shouted Tom, finally looking up at Joe.

"The storm, it's coming back!"

Tom looked at the sky and shrugged. "It's probably just the tail end of it; it'll rain for a minute and then go." He went back to watching the fish.

Joe wasn't quite so sure, but he went along with his older brother, going back to his own fishing while the sky grew darker and darker above them.

The rain continued to pour, heavier now, and Joe kept glancing anxiously at the sky. If the storm was coming back, he didn't think it would be a good idea to stay in the river. They needed to be on the land, where they could easily run for shelter.

"Tom…"

Tom rolled his eyes at Joe. "It'll be over soon, don't worry."

Just then, however, a bolt of lightning flashed down to the ground, lighting up the dreary sky for a second in a brilliant white. The boys were so shocked that they still hadn't moved when the sound of thunder rumbled in the distance a few seconds later.

Then, frantically, Joe turned to his brothers. "*Now* do you believe me?"

Tom nodded, his face extremely pale. "We need to get back to that shed. Leave the fish here, and we can use our spears to help us get out of the river. Come on!"

The three brothers started wading out of the water, using the pointy ends of their sticks to dig into the river bed and help them along.

They were almost out when Joe slipped, falling down into the water and crying out for help. Tom quickly went back for him, pulling him up as Joe gasped for air.

The rain was now coming thick and fast, the wind howling around them as they struggled through the water.

"We're nearly there!" shouted Tom, loudly so the others could hear him.

A few seconds later, the three brothers were scrambling up the river bank, grabbing onto clumps of grass to try and help them up.

They were just metres away from the old shed when another bolt of lightning hit a nearby tree, and before they knew what was happening, a large, thick branch had fallen down in front of them, blocking their way.

By now the rain had turned to hail, and with their vision impaired, it took Tom and Jack a few seconds to realise that Joe wasn't running alongside them. Looking back, they saw him bent over, next to the fallen branch.

"Joe!" shouted Jack. "What's wrong?"

Joe was reaching out for his foot as tears ran down his face. "The branch fell on it! I think it's broken!"

Between them, Tom and Jack lifted their little brother and carried him over to the shed.

Soon, they were all inside, shivering from the cold and soaked to the skin.

"Are you OK?" asked Tom, frowning at Joe in concern.

"I'm not sure… I think I need a doctor."

Jack nodded, while the thunder continued to rumble in the distance. "We'll have to wait until the storm is over."

Even though he was in pain, Joe managed a small laugh. "I told you it was coming back!"

Tom smiled sheepishly. "You're right, we must have been in the eye of the storm."

"What's that?" asked Joe.

"It's when everything goes calm for a little while after a storm, but really it's just the middle of it."

"So it will end soon?" asked Jack, who was also very worried about his little brother.

"It should," said Tom, and at that very moment, the sound of the hail clattering against the roof of the shed started to slow down.

They waited another minute and then Tom peered his head around the shed door to see the sun shining once again. "It's over!"

Relieved, the three brothers left the shed, Tom and Jack helping Joe as they walked back to the gypsy camp.

ZingGo was both pleased and worried when he saw them. "What happened?"

"A tree branch fell on Joe's foot," explained Tom. "You said you had a doctor here; could you find him please?"

Happy to help, ZingGo agreed, and soon Joe was being treated by the gypsy's doctor. He helped wrap his foot up and told Joe he would need to rest it for several days. Luckily, it wasn't broken, just sprained.

"We still need to get home first," said Tom, trying to think what to do.

"I can drive you home," said ZingGo, pointing at his caravan. "My house has wheels!"

The boys laughed while they gratefully accepted his offer, and soon they were on their way home.

"Well, that cross-country run didn't go quite as planned!" said Jack.

"Yes, I think I'll give up running for a little while," said Joe.

"And fishing," added Tom, as ZingGo pulled up outside their little cottage in the woods.

On seeing the caravan, their parents came running out and their mother asked, "What have you done now?" as she took in Joe's wrapped-up foot.

Joe looked at his brothers and laughed. "Well, we went for a cross-country run…"

Tom smiled. "But it turns out…"

Jack laughed. "The country was cross with us!"

They all laughed, and Joe hobbled into the cottage where he could rest his foot, far away from the eye of the storm.

The Fairies of the Wood

Tom, Jack and Joe loved their house in the middle of the woods (where they lived with their mother and father), but even more than that, they loved adventures. They loved going on adventures, they loved telling people about their adventures, and they loved hearing about the adventures that others went on.

The thing they loved most, however, was exploring the woods around their home; even though they'd lived there all their lives, they were always finding new paths and new places.

One morning, Jack and Joe found their brother just outside the house. He was sitting on a bench and writing in his diary – he always wrote down their adventures, to make sure they wouldn't forget a single thing.

"Tom!" yelled Jack enthusiastically. "We want to go on another adventure."

"Yes," agreed Joe. "It's been a long time since the last one."

Tom laughed, shaking his head. "It's been a week, and I'm not sure today would be such a good day for it." He looked up at the sky: it was a cold, foggy morning, and you could feel the damp in the air as it came down around you.

"Oh, come on," said Joe. "It's just a bit of fog, we'll be fine." He held up his rucksack and gestured at the other two bags that were on the ground by Jack. "We've packed everything we might need, and Mum and Dad have packed us plenty of food."

Tom thought for a couple of seconds, then gave into his brothers. "Fine, we'll go!" he said, smiling, as he put his diary and pen into his rucksack.

After saying goodbye to their parents, they headed off into the woods.

"Where shall we go?" asked Tom.

"I'm not sure," said Joe. "We could find the river again?"

"Or go and say hello to the gypsies again?" suggested Jack. They'd met ZingGo and his family there, and they now thought of all of the gypsies as their friends.

"Whatever we do," said Tom, "we have to stick together." As the oldest of the boys, he was always looking out for them – he had their best interests at heart, and was always thinking of their safety. He looked up again at the dark, gloomy sky. "We don't want to get separated in this fog."

His brothers agreed, and they carried on through the forest.

They hadn't got very far when Joe suddenly stopped, whispering, "Look over there! There are some deer!" He said it quietly, so he wouldn't frighten the beautiful animals away.

Tom and Jack saw the deer too – there were several of them in a clearing, a family by the looks of it.

They were sniffing at something on the ground, but when they heard Joe take a step towards them, they all ran off into the woods.

"You made them leave!" said Jack, looking disappointed.

"I just wanted to see what they were sniffing at," said Joe, as he walked over to the spot where the deer had been. Looking down, he saw a small, furry animal. "It's a fox!"

The other two ran over, peering down at the little fox on the forest floor.

"Why isn't it running away?" asked Joe, as he kneeled down to get a better look.

"Perhaps it can't. Maybe it's hurt its foot," suggested Tom, who also kneeled down on the ground.

Tentatively, he reached out and patted the fox on its head, and when it didn't seem to be bothered by his presence, he touched the fox's leg, which was sticking out from under it.

The creature immediately yelped.

"It's definitely his leg," said Tom. "What can we do?"

Jack was pacing up and down next to his brothers, thinking. "We should take it to the gypsies; I bet ZingGo would know what to do!"

Tom and Joe agreed, and after taking a blanket out of Tom's rucksack, they carefully moved the injured fox onto it. They then wrapped it up into a little bundle, with the fox's head poking out of one end.

"That went pretty well!" said Joe. "I didn't think the fox would be very pleased about us picking him up."

Jack nodded. "He must realise that we're trying to help him."

"OK," said Tom, "Let's go." He then led the way out of the forest and across the fields. They'd found the gypsy camp by accident the first time, but Tom had since memorised where to go.

Eventually, they got to the camp and went up to ZingGo's caravan. He was outside, sitting at a table with a cup of tea.

"Hello!" he shouted, standing up and heading over to the three boys. "It's good to see you." He saw the bundle in Tom's hands and leaned down to inspect it. "What have we got here?"

Tom handed him the blanket. "It's a fox. We found him in the woods and we think his foot is broken. Can you help?"

ZingGo took the fox in the blanket over to the table, where he placed it down gently. He then unwrapped the blanket and inspected the fox's leg, while the little creature peered up at him with big, round eyes.

"It looks broken," said ZingGo. "It's going to take weeks to heal, but while it's healing, the poor fox won't be able to find any food or look after himself properly."

Joe looked down at the fox. "Is there nothing else we can do to help?"

ZingGo thought for a moment, and then his daughter, Zanfaya, came over to see what was happening.

"What about the fairies?" she asked her father. "I'm sure they could help, if they could find them."

ZingGo nodded as he glanced over at the three boys.

"The fairies?" asked Tom, intrigued. He could tell that his brothers were also waiting in anticipation to see what the gypsies would say next.

"Yes," said ZingGo. "There's a group of fairies who live in the woods, and they have access to a well that is said to be filled with healing water. I'm sure that if you got some of the water, you could help this little fox."

Tom couldn't believe what he was hearing. "Fairies? But we've never seen any fairies in the wood!" he shouted.

"Ah," said ZingGo, "that is probably because you weren't looking for them. I can give you a map to show where you can find them, but you'll have to go down the river for a while first. You can borrow our canoes if you wish."

The three boys looked at each other and nodded. This sounded like an adventure they couldn't refuse!

*****

Half an hour later, the three boys were standing at the edge of the river with ZingGo. He'd loaned them three of the gypsies' canoes and had given them a map, which looked extremely old. He'd also given them a jar each with a removable lid, so that when they found the fairy well, they'd be able to bring the water back to the camp.

"There you go," said ZingGo, pointing downstream. "Just head straight down there and when you get to the fork in the river, make sure you paddle over to the right. Then you should start to see the fairies."

The three boys thanked the gypsy and climbed into their canoes, grasping their paddles. Their father had taught them all how to paddle and steer canoes a couple of summers ago, and they all felt relatively confident that they'd be able to go down the right part of the river.

ZingGo waved them goodbye, telling them that he'd look after the fox until they returned, and then he left to go back to the camp.

Just as the three boys were ready to go, a large insect landed on Joe's face, causing him to jump up and capsize the canoe. He landed in the river with a wet splosh.

Tom and Jack tried to keep straight faces as they helped their brother back into his canoe, but that didn't last very long – soon they were laughing so hard they couldn't breathe.

"Hey!" said Joe. "We need to focus on finding the fairies, not on laughing at me!"

Tom and Jack apologised, and soon the three of them were gliding down the river. It was still foggy, which created a thick layer of mist over the water, but they had enough light to see where they were going.

Soon, they came to the fork in the river, and all three of them paddled madly to the right, trying to avoid being taken down the left path by the current. They all just about made it, but it tired them out a lot; paddling was hard work.

"How do we know when we're in the right place?" shouted Joe to his brothers.

"I don't know," said Tom, trying to look at the map while still paddling. "It should be around here somewhere."

"There!" shouted Jack, pointing up at the trees on the bank. "There's something on those branches!"

Tom and Joe looked over at the trees, and sure enough, there were some small, human-like creatures perched amongst the leaves. They emitted a pale yellow light, something that glowed in the gloom of the fog. They were obviously very magical creatures.

Signalling to his brothers, Tom steered his canoe over to the bank and hopped out, pulling the boat up after him. Jack and Joe did the same, making sure the canoes were safely on the grass before turning towards the trees.

"They're moving!" shouted Joe. "Quick, let's follow them!"

They watched as the three glowing lights jumped off the trees and scampered into the forest, then the three brothers ran after them as quickly as they could.

They followed them deep into the woods, and as they went, they saw more and more pale yellow lights up high in the trees. There were fairies everywhere – hundreds of them, more than the three boys ever thought possible. Despite the fog, they lit up the woods as if it were a bright summer's day.

The boys started laughing as they watched the fairies dart about above them, and they swore they could hear some chuckling coming from up in the trees, as if the fairies were playing a game with them.

"Wait!" shouted Tom, who was almost out of breath from running. "We need your help! We have an injured fox and we would like something to heal him!"

The chuckling in the trees stopped, and it was soon followed by a low, murmuring hum.

The brothers stopped to catch their breath, waiting for some kind of response.

Then, suddenly, all of the pale yellow lights congregated in one place, and they all started moving off in the same direction, quicker than ever before.

Taking a deep breath, the boys followed the mass of lights through the forest, jumping over tree roots and ducking under branches, and before they knew what was happening, they felt themselves falling down, down, down.

All three brothers shouted out in surprise as they found themselves hurtling down a dank, dark chute, and before long, they landed with a soft thump on a huge pile of leaves.

"Where are we?" asked Joe, looking around him in confusion.

"Down a hole," said Jack, as he brushed himself off. "Down a very big hole."

"But what about the fairies? They were going to help us!" said Joe in a panic. "We need to help out that poor fox."

Tom thought for a moment. "Well, we were following the fairies when we fell down here; perhaps they meant for us to come here. ZingGo mentioned a well – perhaps it's around here somewhere."

"It's ever so dark down here," said Joe. "Why don't you look in your rucksack, Tom? There should be a torch packed in there."

Tom was just scrambling around in his bag for his torch when a pale yellow light flickered on in front of them.

"It's a fairy!" shouted Joe, excited again.

They could just about make out the outline of the small creature hovering in front of them, and then it slowly started flying off, down a tunnel.

Tom immediately started following it – the fairy was obviously trying to tell them which way to go, and if they kept up with it, they wouldn't even need a torch; they could just use the light of the fairy.

They carried on walking for several minutes, and soon they emerged into a large, underground cavern. They could see how big it was due to the hundreds of fairies who lit up the area around them, flying and darting about like they'd done in the trees in the woods.

"Hello," said Tom tentatively. "I'm Tom and these are my brothers, Jack and Joe. We're here because ZingGo the gypsy told us of your magic well."

One of the fairies – one whose light seemed a little brighter than the others – flew over to them, and at last the boys could have a good look at one of the creatures. It basically looked like a human, but smaller, with sharp, pointed features – their ears and noses were especially pointy – and delicate white wings. The pale yellow glow came from all around them, as if they were being lit up from the inside.

When it spoke, its voice was high-pitched, but quiet, like a whisper. "We can help you. We're friends of the gypsies, and we're glad they brought you here."

Joe was looking around him in awe at the fairy in front of him, and at all the rest of them, hovering around in the big space.

Jack nudged Tom, whispering, "Say something!"

Tom cleared his throat, answering the fairy with, "Thank you. We've got some jars, so if you could please show us where the well is…"

"Of course," said the fairy leader, without hesitation. "If you'd like to follow me, I will take you to the magic water."

With that, the fairy flew off, and the boys followed behind.

They hadn't gone very far when the fairy stopped, pointing down at a hole in the ground. "There is the magic well; its water will heal any living creature, just soak the wounded spot in the water and wait for several hours."

The boys thanked him, then lent down to the water to fill up their jars. It didn't take very long, and when they were finished, they put the jars into their rucksacks to keep them safe.

"We don't know how to thank you," said Tom, as he stood up again. "We weren't even sure if you existed; we live in these woods and we've never seen you before."

The fairy leader chuckled. "That's because you weren't *aware* that we existed. Now, you will see us – if you wish to, of course."

Joe was smiling widely. "Of course we wish to!"

Jack agreed, nodding his head enthusiastically.

"Then it is settled," said the fairy leader.

"Thank you," said Tom again, before looking around him at the gaping cavern they were in. "Er… just one question. How do we get out of here?" He thought of the long, long chute they'd fallen down to get here – he didn't feel like climbing up there to get back to the woods!

The fairy leader smiled. "With magic, of course! Now, if you three will stand together – that's it, huddle together – then I will be able to get you back up above ground again." He paused for a moment while the boys moved closer. "Now, you will come and see us again, won't you?"

The boys nodded as the fairy leader threw some fairy dust over the three of them.

"Goodbye, and good luck with helping your animal friend!"

And then – just like that – the three boys were back at the edge of the river, where ZingGo had dropped them off earlier. The three canoes were also there, as if they'd been there all along.

"Wow!" said Joe, looking around him in amazement. "That was actual magic!"

"I'm glad we didn't have to climb up that chute," said Jack, as Tom nodded in agreement.

The three boys looked around, amazed that they were not only back on firm ground, but back on the other side of the river as well.

Confused, Tom opened his rucksack and dug inside until he found the jar. It was full of water – a water that gave off a pale, yellow glow.

Tom sighed in relief. Part of him thought that he must have imagined the whole thing!

Jack and Joe checked their rucksacks, and they too found their jars, full of the magic fairy water. The three boys laughed; the whole thing had been like something out of – well, out of a fairy tale!

Thinking now of the fox, Tom, Jack and Joe put the canoes in a safe place behind some bushes and headed back along the meadows, eventually arriving at the gypsy camp.

ZingGo and Zanfaya – who'd been waiting for them – ran over straight away.

"Did you get it?" asked ZingGo.

"Did you see the fairies?" asked Zanfaya.

The boys nodded, holding up their jars of glowing water, then they all walked over to the fox, who was still sitting on the table. The gypsies had given him a bowl of water and a bowl of food, filled with vegetables and fruit.

Carefully, Tom opened his jar of water and took the fox's paw, dipping it into the jar. ZingGo then brought over some bandages, and Tom soaked these in water too before wrapping them around the fox's leg.

"The fairies said to leave it a few hours," Tom informed them, and ZingGo nodded.

"He can stay here, and you're welcome to stay for some food while we wait. My wife is cooking dinner as we speak."

The three boys accepted gratefully – they were extremely hungry after their adventure – and sat down next to the table, where they could occasionally reach out and stroke the fox.

"What shall we do with the rest of this magic water?" asked Joe, holding up his and Jack's jars. "Do you want to keep them for the camp, ZingGo?"

The gypsy smiled at him. "I'll keep one, but I think you boys should keep the other."

"Why's that?" asked Tom.

"Well," said ZingGo. "I'm sure it'll come in handy; I know how much you boys like to get in trouble!"

The three brothers laughed at this, and Tom could have sworn that the fox gave a little chuckle too.

The Cave Of Gold

Now we return to the wood, and to the thatched cottage where Tom, Jack and Joe lived with their parents, Rosie and George.

It was a cold winter's day in the middle of December, and the weather had turned overnight; snow had been falling down for the past eight hours, and when morning came round, there was a white blanket of snow all around.

The three brothers woke up early, and stretching their arms out, they walked towards the large windows in the bedroom they shared with each other.

Looking out at the snow white ground, Tom grinned excitedly – he loved snow. "Looks like Jack Frost has been round with his paintbrush!" he shouted to the others.

Joe nodded, pointing at one of the nearby trees. "You can see some robins on that branch!"

"Looks like a picture out of a fairy tale," answered Jack.

"Or a Christmas card!" piped up Tom.

The three boys stared out at the picturesque scene for a while longer, before going downstairs and having breakfast. Their mum had put on a huge spread – toast and jam, cereal, orange juice, tea… there was enough food there to feed an army.

After they'd finished, Tom leant back in his chair. "Shall we go outside? Make the most of the snow?"

His two brothers agreed, and walking into the hall, they wrapped themselves up for the cold: coats, scarves, hats and gloves were put on by all.

After saying goodbye to their parents (and filling up their backpacks with supplies), the three of them headed off into the woods, their shoes crunching on the crisp, white snow.

Pretending to tie his shoelace, Joe fell back from his brothers, leaning down and gathering up as much snow as he could, forming it into two perfect balls. Then, as quiet as he could, he ran up behind Tom and Jack and threw the snowballs at the backs of their necks.

Tom turned around, his eyes wide. "Right, you are so dead, little brother!" he shouted, as Joe ran away, laughing.

Jack ran after him, slipping in the snow as he went, and Tom – who'd been right behind him – fell over Jack as well.

Joe started laughing even more – it was usually him that got the short straw, and now it was his brothers on the end of the joke! It made a change, and now the shoe was on the other foot.

"Come and get me if you can!" shouted Joe gleefully, as he ran in circles around his two brothers.

Tom helped Jack to his feet as he yelled, "You can run, little brother, but you can't hide!"

Just as Joe was running past them, Jack reached out and grabbed him, pulling him down to the ground. "Got you!" he shouted, as he started to tickle his younger brother.

Tom joined in with the tickling – they knew Joe was ticklish under his arms, and even with his large coat on, he was laughing and squirming about in the snow.

"Stop, stop! I surrender!" shouted Joe in between giggles, and all three of the brothers laughed.

They lay on the snow for a moment to try and catch their breath, unaware of the boy who was watching them from behind a tree – they'd been having so much fun, they hadn't seen or heard him appear.

After a few minutes, Joe picked himself up off the ground and brushed the snow off his coat. When he looked up, he noticed the boy standing there, and as he walked over to him, he introduced himself.

"Hello, my name is Joe. And these are my two brothers – Tom and Jack."

"How do you do?" said the boy. "My name is Harry."

"Nice to meet you, Harry," Joe said.

"Do you live here?" asked Tom. "In the woods?" He was intrigued as he'd never seen Harry around before.

"Yes," Harry replied. "I live with my mum, not too far from here." He pointed into the woods. "Come on, I'll show you."

The four of them set off in the direction of Harry's house, taking breaks every so often to throw snowballs at each other.

"I like this time of year because you can see all the wildlife," said Harry, as a squirrel ran past his feet and up a nearby tree. "They're so visible against the snow!"

The brothers agreed with their new friend, and as they continued on their way, Joe started to see something in the white powder on the ground. "What are these?" he asked, pointing at the marks. "Are these paw prints?"

Harry looked down at them as well. "I think they're badger tracks!" he said. "There are a lot of badgers around here."

"I hope we see one!" said Joe, who also loved animals of all kinds.

Before they all knew it, they came to a log cabin in the woods. It was quite small and rickety, like something out of a fairy tale, and its single chimney had a puff of smoke floating out of the top of it.

"Welcome to my home," Harry announced. "Looks like my mum's cooking, but we can go up to my room."

The three brothers looked around in wonder as they made their way into the cabin. It was much smaller than their house, but it had a lot more character – little knick-knacks were dotted around everywhere, and each wall was covered in paintings and photographs of the surrounding woods.

The brothers could tell that Harry and his mother didn't have much in the way of money, but they thought their home was just great.

"It needs a lot of repairs," said Harry, shrugging. He seemed a little embarrassed by this, but then he brightened up as he ran up the stairs, two at a time. "My room's up here!" he called, as the three brothers followed.

Harry's room was just as interesting as the rest of the house, as it was filled with fascinating objects of all shapes and sizes.

"I'm a collector," said Harry, picking up a large, multi-coloured feather. "Though most of this stuff was my grandfather's."

Tom, Jack and Joe started wandering around the room, picking up smooth pebbles and rocks that shone like crystals.

In a chest of old-looking papers, Joe pulled out what seemed to be a map. It was drawn on old parchment, and it showed the location of something in the woods. At the top, in large, fancy handwriting, were the words: 'The Cave Of Gold'. Excited, he peered into the bottom of the chest to see a small gold medallion, supposedly from the same place.

"Wow," said Joe, showing the map to his brothers. "Was this your grandfather's too?"

"Oh yes," said Harry, his eyes lighting up. "That's where that gold's from – or at least, that's what he told me.

I think the medallion is worth quite a bit of money, but it's the only one I have, and I'd never get rid of it."

"Have you ever been to the cave yourself?" asked Joe. "Tried to find more gold?"

Harry shook his head. "I've always wanted to try and find the cave, but I didn't want to go on my own."

Jack and Tom looked at the map over Joe's shoulder, getting the same idea at exactly the same time.

"We should go and find it now!" said Jack. "We've got supplies – we never leave home without our backpacks. We've got food and water and everything."

Excited now, the four friends took the map and walked back down the stairs, Harry calling 'goodbye' to his mum as they left.

Once they were outside the house, Tom took a compass out of his pocket and found due north. He then turned the map around accordingly and stared at it for a few moments. "It's this way!" he shouted, walking off from the group.

The others ran to keep up with him, laughing when Joe tripped and fell over in the snow.

"At least I had a soft landing!" he cried, as he rolled onto his back and made a snow angel.

"Come on," said Tom. "We want to get to the cave before it's dark so we can find our way back again!" He rushed off without waiting for Joe to get up, but Harry stayed behind to give his new friend a hand.

Around a couple of hours later – after a lot of turns and wrong turns – the four friends arrived in a clearing in the woods.

"According to the map, the cave should be here," said Tom, frowning.

"I don't see any cave," said Joe.

"Me neither," said Jack. "Is this definitely a real map?"

Harry nodded enthusiastically. "My grandfather told me he'd been to the cave as a boy. It definitely exists."

"Let me have a look at the map," said Joe, reaching out to take it off Tom.

Tom laughed. "You think you can find some sort of secret code on it?" Jack laughed with him.

A little annoyed – his older brothers were always picking on him! – Joe took the map off Tom without saying anything. After studying it for a minute or so, he nodded and gave it back.

Then he walked over to the edge of the clearing, where there were several huge ferns blocking the path.

"In here!" he cried, as he started pushing through the leaves.

Confused, Tom, Jack and Harry followed him, making their way through the foliage just behind Joe.

After a few minutes, Joe came to the end of the tunnel of ferns and was met with a large rock face. "It's here!" he shouted, as the others emerged from the leaves. "There's a hole there we can squeeze through!"

Tom and Jack were amazed, and vowed to never make fun of Joe again. Or, at least for a little while.

"Wait," said Tom, as he put his backpack on the floor and pulled out three torches. He handed them out while Jack brought a lantern out of his own backpack.

Then, taking deep breaths to calm their nerves, they entered the cave one by one.

It was dark and damp in the cave, and Tom – who was leading the way – had to crouch to get through the small tunnel at the opening. "Just a bit further!" he shouted back to the others as he continued scrambling down the tunnel, and before he knew it, he was stepping out into a vast, echoing cavern, one so big the light from his torch didn't even reach the far side.

The others climbed out of the tunnel then, gasped as they saw the cave they were now in – it was huge!

"Wow," said Harry. "I had no idea it would be like this. I wonder if there's any gold here?"

Shining his torch around, Tom shrugged. "There's only one way to find out. Let's start exploring!"

Joe laughed in delight as he started walking around the edge of the cave, shining his torch on the walls and looking for signs of another passageway.

"This reminds me of the fairy cave," said Jack, as he followed his little brother. "Although without the fairies! We could sure use their light right about now!"

The others agreed, telling Harry about their adventure with the fairies as they carried on walking.

All of a sudden, Joe stopped. "I found something!" he said, as the others all huddled round and pointed their lights at the wall. "It looks like a lever or something…" He turned to face Tom. "Should I pull it?"

Tom thought for a moment. "We don't know what it will do, and it could be dangerous…"

"Or it could lead to a room full of gold," said Jack, grinning. "It can't be that dangerous if Harry's grandfather came here, and got out, *and* left the map for Harry to find."

The others agreed, and after only a slight hesitation, Tom pulled on the lever.

There were a few moments of silence, and then a low, rumbling sound reached their ears, getting louder and louder as the seconds ticked by.

"What is that?" asked Joe, just as a panel in the wall started to open, making a loud, creaking sound that echoed around the cave.

Before they knew it, swarms of bats and rats came flying and scuttling out of the opening in the wall, making the friends fall over in surprise.

Joe laughed as a rat ran over his legs, tickling him with his little rodent paws.

A bat got stuck in Tom's hair, and he shrieked like a girl as he tried to get it out – something that the others found hilarious.

Soon, the bats and rats had all gone – disappeared into other corners of the cave – and the four friends looked at each other, laughing.

"I wasn't expecting that!" said Harry.

"Well, you did say you liked seeing the wildlife this time of year," said Jack, laughing.

Joe also laughed as he peered into the opening in the cave wall. "Hey, I think this leads to another room – we can just about fit through it, I think!"

Checking there weren't any more little furry surprises, Tom led the way again, climbing in through the hole and scooting down yet another little tunnel. The others followed, Joe shouting out in pain as he banged his head on the roof of the small space.

Soon, however, they were all out of the tunnel and shining their torches and the lantern around another large chamber.

From here they could hear the sound of rushing water, and following the noise, the four friends soon came to an underground river. Water was trickling over the rocks in the walls – like tiny underground waterfalls – and past the river, they could just about make out a glinting pile of gold.

"There!" said Joe, pointing into the distance. "That must be it!"

"But how do we cross the river?" asked Jack, scratching his head.

Harry started walking along the underground river bank, and after a few minutes, he called out to the others, "Here! There's a rope bridge!"

The three brothers ran over to him, sighing when they saw the bridge – they hadn't had much luck with ropes over water in the past, and this bridge looked highly unstable.

"I'll go first," said Harry, and before the others even had a chance to respond, he was crawling over the ropes, his trousers almost touching the water as he scrambled across. "I made it!" he shouted from the other bank, and with new found hope, Tom and Jack followed after him.

When it got to Joe's turn, however, he was so nervous that he trembled as he went over, and as he wasn't concentrating, he lost his footing, slipping into the river below. "Help!" he shouted desperately, as his torch fell into the water and got washed away.

Tom, Jack and Harry rushed back to the bridge, reaching out their hands as Joe tried to cling onto the rope. His legs were fully in the water now, getting soaked as he tried to pull himself out of it. "I'm slipping!" he yelled, trying to remain calm.

"Hold onto my hand!" shouted Tom, as he grabbed his little brother's wrist. Harry and Jack grabbed Tom round the waist, and between the three of them, they pulled Joe out of the water and onto the other side of the river bank.

Joe lay on the ground for a moment, catching his breath. "Thanks, guys!" he said. "We never have much luck with water, do we?"

The brothers started laughing at that, a sound that echoed around the entire cave.

"Now, the gold!" shouted Harry, as he ran over to the glittering pile, the others following quickly behind.

What they saw was a pile of gold medallions, the same as the one Harry had in his room, and they quickly started gathering them up, putting them in their pockets and backpacks, wherever they could.

"These are pieces of history," said Tom, as he held one up to the light from his torch. "We should take them to the police. If they don't belong to anyone, they might get put into a museum."

The others agreed, and soon they were laden down with the little gold coins.

They were just about to leave when something ran over Joe's foot, and thinking it was another rat, he glanced down.

It wasn't a rat, however, but a badger, and he had a gold medallion in his mouth!

"Look!" shouted Joe, as the badger scuttled away.

The four friends followed him, through the cave and around a corner, and that's when they saw it: an entire chamber filled with not only gold, but pieces of silver and jewels in every colour as well.

They stared at it in awe, no one wanting to say anything for a good few moments.

"We should let someone know about this," said Tom, still staring at the glittering room. "It's all too beautiful to be left in a dank, dark cave!"

The others nodded, and with the decision made, they started retracing their steps. This time, they made it across the river without incident, and soon they were emerging back into the woods, surprised to find it was still light.

A couple of hours later, they were at the police station, telling them of their discovery and showing them the gold medallions they'd brought back with them.

"We thought the treasure could go in some museum," said Harry, who knew the Chief of Police, John Hatfield, as he was a friend of his mother's.

John smiled at Harry. "I'm sure it could; it's definitely solid gold," he said, as he held one of the medallions up to the light. "Thank you for telling us, boys. For your trouble, you can each keep the gold you carry on you now – think of it as a finder's fee. We'll go back to the cave and retrieve the rest."

"Really?" asked Harry, his eyes wide.

"Yes," replied John. "I know it's been tough for your mum, Harry, and this will help her out a great deal."

The boys – who couldn't believe their luck – thanked the police chief and left the station, heading back to the woods and their homes.

Thinking of the cabin Harry shared with his mum – and all the repairs that needed doing – the brothers glanced at each other, and realising they were thinking the same thing, they all nodded.

"Harry," said Tom. "We'd like you to keep this gold – your mum needs it more than us, and if it wasn't for your map, we'd never even know the gold and all those jewels existed."

Harry thanked them, not knowing what else to say, until he thought back to their time in the cave. "Well, really, we should thank that badger!"

The three brothers laughed as Joe said, "You sure do like your wildlife, Harry!"

The Mystery Island of the Lost Diamonds

Tom, Jack and Joe lived in a little cottage in the heart of the woods, along with their parents, Rosie and George. They often went on adventures together and met new, interesting people, but they didn't often get many visitors.

This, however, was about to change.

The boys' father, George, was outside the front of their cottage, watering the hanging baskets and other flowers that were dotted around in various different-sized plant pots. He was a keen gardener, and he just loved watering his flowers.

The sound of approaching footsteps made him stop what he was doing, and looking up, he saw a boy walking towards the house – an Indian boy.

"Hello!" he said politely. "You must be Cumbow." His sons had told him about their adventures with the Indian boy – who they'd met at the Indian camp – and there was no one else this boy could be.

"Yes," replied Cumbow. "You must be Tom, Jack and Joe's father. It's nice to meet you." He smiled up at the man as he came to a stop in front of the cottage.

"Likewise," said George, shaking the boy's free hand (his other was hidden behind his back). "The boys have told me so much about you; they'll be delighted when they see you've come to visit."

"I hope so," said Cumbow, finishing the handshake and bringing his other hand out from behind his back. "I've brought some fish for you all. I caught them this morning."

George was about to thank Cumbow for his thoughtful gift when his eldest son, Tom, popped his head around the corner.

"Cumbow!" he cried gleefully. "I thought I recognised that voice! Long time no see!"

"Yes," said Cumbow, smiling. "I thought I'd surprise you."

Tom walked over to Cumbow and high fived him, and a few seconds later Jack and Joe appeared, doing the same thing.

George took the fish off Cumbow and went into the house, and after the boys had caught up with their friend, their mum, Rosie, shouted out to them from the kitchen.

"Boys! Dinner's ready!" she called in her singsong voice. "We've got some lovely fish thanks to Cumbow. Would you like to stay, dear?"

Cumbow nodded enthusiastically, and soon all four boys were sitting down with Rosie and George to eat a slap up meal.

"You won't believe what happened a few weeks ago," said Joe enthusiastically. "We found a cave of gold!"

"And loads of jewels too!" added Jack, who was just as eager to impress their Indian friend as his brother was.

"Really?" asked Cumbow, impressed. "How did you find that?" He'd never even heard of a cave of gold around here.

"Our friend Harry had a map. It was his grandfather's," explained Tom. "You should see his room; it's full of all kinds of wonderful things."

"Oh, yes!" shouted Joe, jumping up from his chair. "We could go on another adventure, with you and Harry! What do you say, Cumbow? For old times' sake?"

Cumbow nodded. "Yes, definitely. It would be nice to explore some new paths, and to meet your friend Harry."

"Let's go tomorrow! Can you stay the night, Cumbow?" asked Jack.

"I'd love to," he said, looking at the boys' parents. "If it's not too much trouble? I told my grandfather where I was coming."

Rosie smiled. "No trouble at all. Say, if you're going over to Harry's I think I'll come too. I want to meet his mum and see how she's doing."

George nodded in agreement. Harry lived in a tiny cottage with just his mum, and Rosie had wanted to meet her ever since she found out.

So, it was settled. In the morning, they would set off to Harry's house, and then hopefully set off to pastures new. They couldn't wait to see what kind of adventure awaited them next.

*****

The next morning, the boys, their parents, and Cumbow set off bright and early, trekking through the woods until they got to Harry's little shack. As they approached it they could see smoke coming out of the chimney, and soon they were all inside, the boys introducing Harry and his mum to Cumbow and their parents.

"Why don't you boys run and play upstairs while the grownups have a cup of tea?" asked Harry's mum, smiling. Her name was Jenny.

The boys didn't have to be told twice, and they all ran up the stairs two at a time, bursting into Harry's room, which itself was bursting with all kinds of strange and fascinating artefacts.

"This is it!" shouted Harry, as he held up a large gold coin and a map. "This map is what led us to the cave, and it was full of these coins, as well as jewels of all shapes and sizes."

"Wow," said Cumbow, as he looked at the map and the coin. "Do you have anything else like this? We want to go on another adventure!"

Harry thought for a moment, glancing around his room at the various pictures and objects. "Oh!" he said, before running over to the chest where he'd got the map from. "There is something else my grandfather left me. I don't know what it means as I've never figured it out. But we could try, together?"

Intrigued, all of the boys gathered around Harry as he pulled what looked like an old scroll out of the chest. It was yellow with age and delicate as he unravelled it, and he cleared his throat before he started reading:

"There is a land across the sea

Of jewels, rocks, and diamonds three.

Leave the turtle and grab the crow

And diamonds shall be yours to know.

Go straight across for four or five

But don't get lost or take a dive,

Go west on land for two to find

Your fortune, down below, and mined."

Once he'd finished reading, Harry looked up at the others and shrugged.

"It's a riddle!" said Tom excitedly.

Harry nodded. "But a riddle about what? I've never been able to decipher it. I know it says about a land of jewels, and it talks about diamonds, but a riddle doesn't really help, does it? If a land of diamonds really exists, we could do with another map."

The three brothers laughed, but Cumbow was looking into the distance, deep in thought.

"What is it?" asked Jack.

"A land of diamonds…" said Cumbow, frowning. "My tribe speaks of the Island of Lost Diamonds. It's a myth, it goes back hundreds of years. Surely… surely it doesn't exist?"

Joe was grinning in excitement. "Let's take the riddle downstairs! Our dad is *great* at riddles."

Before Harry could stop him, Joe took the scroll off him and ran down the stairs, running into the kitchen and thrusting it into his dad's hands. "Dad, can you help us? We think this is a riddle about the Island of Lost Diamonds. Cumbow's tribe knows about it!"

George opened up the scroll, reading silently to himself while the two women looked over his shoulder, doing the same.

After what seemed like forever, he looked up at his sons and Cumbow (who had all followed Joe downstairs), grinning in triumph. "This riddle is quite simple," he said. "So you've already figured out it's telling you about an island of diamonds?" The boys all nodded. "Well, it tells you how to get there too. Although there is one thing I'm not sure about..." He turned to Harry's mum. "Do the words 'the crow' mean anything to you?"

She looked at him blankly for a moment, but then, suddenly, it came to her. "Yes! It was my grandfather's boat. It's been in our family for years. It's only a small fishing boat, but it was his pride and joy. It's moored at Turtle Bay."

George smiled. "Ah yes, it all makes sense now." He turned back to the boys. "Jewels, rocks and diamonds probably all refer to the same thing, as diamonds can be called jewels and they're also known as rocks. I'm assuming 'leave the turtle' means set out from Turtle Bay, which is about an hour away. Grab the crow must mean go in your grandfather's boat, *The Crow*. Straight across for four or five… that must mean keep going in the water for four or five knots – a nautical mile – and then when you get to the island, head west and look underground for the diamonds – 'down below, and mined' means they'll be in the earth, not on top of it."

Everyone in the room stared at George in awe.

"Wow," said Harry. "So you think it's a real place?"

George shrugged. "It could be. And by the sounds of it – using *The Crow* to mean your grandfather's boat, I'd say the person who gave this scroll to him knew him personally."

"The person who gave it to him could have been a member of my tribe!" shouted Cumbow enthusiastically.

"Do you still have the boat?" Harry asked his mum. "Could we go?"

She thought for a moment. "It's still there, and still seaworthy, but I couldn't let you go on your own."

George stood up then, handing the scroll to Harry and patting Cumbow on the shoulder. "I'll go with them – it'll be a lad's adventure! Just like when I was younger!"

Tom, Jack and Joe stared at their dad. "You went on adventures?" Joe asked.

"All the time!" their father replied, laughing. "When I was your age, I was the king of adventurers!"

*****

An hour or so later, all five boys and George were setting sail on *The Crow*, with the wind in their hair and the fresh sea air filling their lungs. The boat looked a little worse for wear, but the man who'd been looking after it informed them that it was fine to go out in, as long as they knew how to row. It had an engine on (a recent addition), he said, but if it were to stop working, they'd have to paddle their way out of danger.

The boys had grinned at each other at this point – they knew how to row; they loved drifting down the river in canoes.

Now, all five of them were sitting in the boat while the engine whirred them along the water, with George keeping watch as to where they were going. He was counting the knots in his head, calculating the distance they were going by their speed. His sons didn't understand any of it, but they were impressed.

They'd been going for a few hours when the sky started to darken, and looking up at the stormy clouds, George frowned. "We might be in for a bit of a rough one, boys!" he shouted over the roar of the waves.

The boys exchanged nervous looks, and a second later, a huge wave splashed over the side of the boat, drenching them all. Luckily, Harry had left the scroll at home – George had memorised the riddle before they left.

"What do we do?" shouted Tom to his dad.

"Just sit still and don't rock the boat!" he shouted back, as it began to rain down on all of them.

While they'd all brought supplies from Harry's house, none of them had a coat, and they shivered as they got wetter and wetter from the rain.

Joe was looking nervously out at the water – they'd had trouble with water in the past, but a river was very different to the open sea. He was just glad his dad was there.

They all huddled together in the middle of the boat, George holding a blanket over their heads to try and keep the water off. "It looks like it might be one of those freak storms!" he shouted at the boys. "Hopefully it won't last too long!"

The boys nodded, hoping he was right, but a second later, another wave splashed over the boat, showering them all with heavy, salty water. The blanket George had been holding up got washed away, and he grabbed onto the side of the boat to steady himself.

Cumbow looked out at the water, scared about what might happen. He'd never been on the open sea before, and he was starting to wonder if this would all be worth it. What if they didn't even find the island?

Just as he was thinking this, another, even bigger wave swept over the boat, dragging Cumbow out with it. He shouted out for help as he got hauled over the side, and Tom just managed to reach out and grab his hands before he fell into the cold water.

"Quick, help me get him back!" shouted Tom, and his brothers, his dad, and Harry all put their weight together to heave Cumbow back over the boat.

He landed in the bottom of the bow, shivering from the cold, and George pulled another blanket out from his backpack before draping it over him.

The rain was easing off now, and a few minutes later, the storm had ended. The boys couldn't believe it as they looked up at the blue sky and the sun shining down on them – it definitely was a freak storm!

Warming themselves under the sun's rays, they carried on with their journey, making sure they were still going in the same direction as they'd been going before the storm hit. They even managed to have a little boat picnic, with cheese and tomato sandwiches and pop they'd brought from Harry's house.

Then, before they knew it, they spotted some land up ahead.

"The Island of the Lost Diamonds!" shouted Cumbow. "It *does* exist!"

George laughed. "Well, let's see if there actually are any diamonds there first, shall we?"

Soon enough, they were pulling up to the shore of the island and using a rope to anchor their boat to a nearby tree. It was a beautiful beach, and the weather was glorious; the sun was shining off the waves and the white sand. It looked like a picture off a postcard.

"So what do we do now?" asked Joe, clearly excited.

"We head west," said George, taking his compass out of his pocket. "This way, boys. Follow me!"

With that, he headed off the beach and into what looked like a kind of jungle. The boys followed, wondering if they'd come across any wildlife here.

They carried on going for several minutes before Tom broke the silence. "How will we know when we've got there?"

George thought back to the riddle. "It said go for two, which could mean two miles. I'm hoping it'll be obvious when we get there."

They continued on, and thirty minutes later George stopped abruptly, causing all of the boys to run into the back of him.

"Sorry!" he shouted. "But this could be it!"

The boys gathered around, and ahead of them they could see a huge rock. Etched onto it was a symbol, something that looked oddly like a diamond.

"That's it!" shouted Cumbow. "I've seen that symbol before! It's in one of the books written by our tribe!"

Tom, Jack, Joe and Harry looked at the rock in awe – they thought the diamonds would be much harder to find.

"So what do we do now?" asked Joe. "Where are the diamonds?"

George stared intently at the rock. "The riddle said they were down below. Let's see if we can move this boulder – between us, we probably can."

All six of them gathered around the rock, and putting all of their strength and energy into it, they leaned down and pushed against it.

At first it wouldn't budge at all, but after a minute or so of gently rocking it back and forth, the rock rolled away, leaving a gaping hole beneath it.

"Wow," said Harry, as he looked down into the hole. Everyone else was too shocked to speak.

With the sun filtering down into the earth, its rays lit up what looked like hundreds of sparkling white diamonds.

Jack was the first to break the silence. "They're actually here! Do you think we should take them? Who do they belong to?"

George was staring at the jewels, his eyes wide. "It sounds like they might belong to your tribe, Cumbow. Let's load ourselves up with as many as we can, and we'll take them to your camp tomorrow."

The boys did as George said, and soon they were heading back through the jungle, eager to get back to the boat and out on the open sea again (as long as there wasn't another freak storm).

Just as they were about to break through the end of the jungle and onto the beach, however, Tom felt a strange motion next to his head – like someone swiping a hand through the air.

He jumped, shouting out and alerting the others.

When his brothers and friends looked round, they all started laughing.

"Monkey!" shouted Joe, pointing behind Tom's head.

He looked behind him and sure enough, there was a monkey, staring at him in wonder. Tom stared back, and before he knew it the monkey had dropped down to the ground, pushing his little monkey hand into Tom's pocket and pulling out one of the diamonds.

"Hey!" yelled Tom. "He took a diamond!"

Just as he'd finished shouting, another monkey appeared, this time behind Joe. He put his hand into *his* pocket, bringing out another diamond.

"Hey, the monkeys are getting away with my tribe's jewels! Run!" yelled Cumbow, as all the boys ran out of the jungle, laughing.

George joined in with the laughter as they walked across the beach and over to their boat. "Who'd have thought that after everything we've been through to get here, we'd be outsmarted by a couple of monkeys!"

*****

After what seemed like an eternity, the boys and George got back to Harry's house (thankfully with no freak storms in sight), and after they'd stumbled into the living room, they collapsed on the sofas, exhausted.

Jenny and Rosie ran in, eager to hear about their adventure.

"Did you find it?" asked Rosie.

"Were there any diamonds?" asked Jenny. "How was the boat? Did you hit any storms?"

"Did you meet anyone?" asked Rosie, who clearly had so many questions that she didn't even have time to wait for an answer before asking the next.

George held his hands up, laughing. "We'll answer all of your questions in time, but first... how about a cup of tea?"

Everyone laughed at that.

"Yes," said Cumbow, looking around him at his new (and not so new) friends. "After what we've been through, I'd love a cup of tea. A big one, please!"

Joe took one of the diamonds out of his pocket and smiled. "I think with these we'll be able to afford as many cups of tea as we want!"

Rosie and Jenny stared at the diamond, their eyes wide, before Rosie started laughing. "I think we can safely say they were successful...!"

The boys joined in the laughter as Joe added, "And so were the monkeys!"

The Dream World of Make Believe

As we look down at the little cottage in the woods, the brothers Tom, Jack and Joe looked up at the dazzling night sky.

Their bedroom was brilliant for stargazing, with its three large windows and the huge skylight in the centre of their ceiling, and as they lived in the woods, they could see much more of space compared to people who lived in the city – out here, the stars were brighter, the moon seemed bigger, and the distant galaxies called out to them.

The brothers had always been big fans of space, ever since they were little. They'd grown up staring at the planets and the constellations, and they still loved doing so now.

"Look at the stars!" shouted Joe happily as he jumped up and down on his bed. "I've never seen so many before."

"They do seem brighter than usual tonight," agreed Tom, "but they still seem so far away."

"And look at the moon!" added Jack, who was just as excited as his brothers.

The three boys gazed at the moon, amazed at how big it was – usually, it was only half the size. It was a full moon tonight, and if you looked at it closely, you could almost swear there was the face of a man etched onto its white surface.

"The man in the moon," said Joe, as he stared up at it.

They all stood watching it for a while longer, then Tom piped up, "Just think of all the planets out there… there must be millions we haven't seen or even heard of."

"Yes," Joe replied, "and think of all the aliens that must be out there! Wouldn't it be cool to meet them? And explore the strange new worlds?"

George – the boys' dad – chuckled as he entered their bedroom. "Talking about aliens again, are we?"

Jack nodded. "Joe thinks there must be loads of aliens out there." He raised his eyebrows as he spoke – he always thought Joe was stuck in a fantasy land.

"Well," said their dad, "he just might be right. Think of how many planets are out there in the universe… it's highly unlikely that Earth would be the only one with any life on it."

"See! I told you!" shouted Joe gleefully, as he jumped up and down on his bed in excitement, making the bed springs creak. "It would be great to explore one of those planets."

"You might do one day," their mum Rosie said as she entered their bedroom. "But you'd better get down from your bed first," she added, looking at Joe. "Come on, boys, it's time to go to sleep."

Moaning, the boys reluctantly got into their beds, pulling up their covers as their parents went round all the windows, drawing the curtains closed.

George was just about to press the button to make the blind on the skylight come down when Joe piped up, "Please, could you leave it, Dad? I want to see the stars!"

George chuckled. "OK, but don't stay up too late stargazing! I'll see you in the morning."

"Yes, good night, boys," Rosie added.

The three brothers all replied, "Good night!" in unison, and then their parents left, pulling the door closed behind them.

"I'm going to do it," whispered Joe in the semi-darkness, the only light being the moon spilling in through the skylight.

"Do what?" asked Tom. He sounded a little grumpy – he wanted to get to sleep.

"I'm going to go to space!" said Joe, laughing. "And I'm going to meet an alien. Maybe a whole group of aliens."

Jack laughed from beneath his covers. "Sure you are, Joe."

Joe sighed, leaning back against his pillow as he stared up through the skylight at the universe beyond.

One day, he'd go to space – he was sure of it.

*****

A few hours later, Joe was woken by a sound coming from just outside their room – a low, rumbling kind of sound.

Intrigued, he slipped out of bed and ran over to between Jack's and Tom's beds, nudging them until they woke up too.

"What is it?" asked Tom, his voice gruff from sleep.

"Can't you hear that?" asked Joe, as he looked up through the skylight. "It sounds like…"

"A flying saucer!" shouted Jack, as he leapt out of bed, his mouth hanging open. "There's a flying saucer hovering over our house!"

The three boys ran over to the skylight, standing underneath it as a bright white light hovered directly overhead.

"Aliens!" shouted Joe, incredibly excited. "I knew they existed!"

"Yes we exist," a voice floated over to them from the light above. "We are Tockrecons, and we come from the Planet Beyond. Would you like to see it?"

"Yes!" shouted Joe, without any hesitation whatsoever. "Well, if we can come back here afterwards."

"Of course!" came the voice. "Now, close your eyes, and we'll beam you aboard."

The three boys did as they were told, and before they knew it, they were all standing in a silver, circular room. There were three figures in front of them, and although they stood upright like men, they certainly didn't look like any men the boys had ever seen.

In fact, they looked exactly how Joe had imagined aliens would look – large, with long limbs and huge black eyes – but for one difference: they were bright purple.

"I thought aliens were green," said Joe. "Like little green men?"

The three aliens laughed, then one of them – the largest – said, "Our cousins on Planet Further are green, but on Planet Beyond, it's purple all the way! I'm Isron, and these are my brothers, Seavone and Ironson."

Joe smiled happily at the greeting. "I'm Joe, and these are *my* brothers, Tom and Jack."

"Welcome aboard, brothers of Earth," said Seavone. "We're now travelling at light speed through space, and we'll be at Planet Beyond in… about thirty seconds."

"Wow!" said Joe, impressed, before running over to a porthole in the flying saucer's outer wall. From here, it felt like he could see the whole of outer space, and he laughed in delight as they zoomed past endless planets and stars.

"We're here!" shouted Ironson. "Now, close your eyes, and we'll beam you onto the surface of our planet. Don't worry – we have the same air as Earth. It's why we visit your planet so often."

The three boys closed their eyes, and a second later, they were on Planet Beyond.

"Wow," said Jack, as he looked around him.

"This place is unreal!" shouted Tom.

Joe just stared at the landscape, completely speechless – for once in his life.

They were in a forest, but it was unlike any forest they'd ever seen. For one thing, instead of the trees and the grass being different shades of green, they were different shades of purple and pink, and instead of the river (that was rushing through the woods) being a nice light blue, it was a bright red colour, like the poster paint they sometimes used at home.

Tom stepped back as a bright turquoise snake slithered near his foot, and Joe laughed as he saw a stripy red, purple and blue bird fly into the air.

"Your planet is very colourful!" said Jack, smiling at the three aliens in front of them. "I'd love to take a boat out on that red river some time!"

"Boat?" asked Isron.

"Yes, we go on canoes down the river," explained Joe.

"Oh, those things!" replied Seavone, laughing. "Yes, we have 'boats'. Come with us."

The three aliens then led the three brothers over to a metallic silver shed on the river bank. Everything on the planet looked extremely new and clean, and the shed looked very futuristic – it was incredibly sleek and chic.

Isron, Seavone and Ironson disappeared into the shed, and when they came back out, they were each carrying a slim, silver pod-like object.

"These are the boats we have here on Planet Beyond," Seavone explained, as he placed his boat in the water. It stayed where it was on the surface of the river, despite the current running underneath.

Isron and Ironson followed suit, and soon all three of the 'boats' were resting on the river.

"Why aren't they being washed away?" asked Tom, as he crept further towards the river to investigate. It was only when he was a few feet away that he saw they weren't *on* the river at all – they were hovering above it!

"Are these hoverboats?" asked Joe excitedly.

"I suppose you could call them that," said Seavone. "Why don't you each get in?"

The boys did as they were told, and when they were each seated in one of the slim, silver boats, they looked up at the aliens, who were still standing on the banks.

"How do we work them?" asked Tom. "There don't seem to be any controls and we don't have any paddles…"

"You don't need controls or paddles," said Isron. "These boats work with the power of your mind. Just think of what you want to do, and the boat will do it."

Jack laughed – he didn't believe it would work, not with their human brains – but he tried it anyway. Closing his eyes, he pictured himself floating down the river, and straight away, his boat set off, hovering just above the water as he went on his way.

"Wait up!" shouted Tom, as he followed behind.

Joe – who had got distracted and had been imagining himself as a big purple alien – was the last to set off, and he tried to catch up with his two brothers.

The journey was wonderful.

Even though the river was red, they could still see their reflections in it, and as they continued down their path, a multitude of brightly coloured fish jumped out of the river beside their boats.

One group of fish were bright red, with green flashing lights spread over their bodies.

"They're like Christmas fish!" Joe shouted, grinning at them as they went on their way.

Joe was so busy looking at the fish, in fact, that he stopped concentrating on what he was doing, and just as he was thinking what it must be like to be a fish, his boat stopped abruptly, tipping him out into the water and hovering off without him.

"Help!" Joe spluttered, as he tried to swim to the bank. "Help me!" He could see his two brothers further upstream, but there was no way they'd be able to get back to him in their boats.

Unless...

Tom heard his brother shouting from behind him, and he had exactly the same thought as Joe had just had. Closing his eyes, he concentrated as hard as he could, picturing himself floating against the current in his hoverboat and picking Joe up, saving him from the water.

When he opened his eyes, he was heading towards his little brother, and Jack was beside him, doing the same thing in his own hoverboat.

They flew over to Joe, leaning down and picking him up. He climbed onto Jack's hoverboat, gasping for air, and looked up at his brothers. "Thanks."

"I think we'd better get these boats back to the aliens, what do you say?" asked Jack. The others agreed.

Before long, they were climbing onto the bank where Isron, Seavone and Ironson stood.

"I'm sorry," said Joe. "But I lost your boat. It threw me into the river and then carried on going!"

Isron looked at the water thoughtfully. "Yes, sorry about that. Some of the hoverboats have a life of their own. He'll go on his little trip down the river then he'll bring himself back. He always does."

"How about some food?" asked Isron, as they walked away from the river.

"Oh, yes please!" shouted Joe. "I never say no to food."

The aliens laughed, and soon the brothers were being shown into another large, silver structure. There were a lot of screens dotted around, blocking off different parts of the room, and every single surface was shiny and clean. The boys realised they could see their reflections everywhere.

"I apologise if it takes a little while to get the meal ready," said Isron. "We're not used to guests."

With that, he walked over to what appeared to be a little kitchen area. He pressed a button on a small round object, and a tiny blue cube popped up from the top of it.

He then brought this cube over to the table, which was laid with several plates and glasses.

He placed the cube on one of the plates, and the boys watched in amazement as it started expanding, getting bigger and bigger and turning into a giant cake in front of their very eyes.

Seavone and Ironson came over to the table with several other cubes of different colours, and these turned into sandwiches, jugs of pop, chocolates and fruit.

"Wow," said Joe. "That was the quickest cooking I've ever seen!"

"Oh good!" said Isron. "Our normal cube maker is broken, and we were worried this would be too long to wait for your food."

The three boys laughed as they dug into the meal. Everything tasted wonderful, but it was a little confusing. The chocolates tasted of cake, the cake of fruit, and the fruit of chocolate!

They weren't sure what filling was in the sandwiches, but it was incredibly tasty, and the pop was one of the sweetest, most delicious things they'd ever had.

"Can we live here?" asked Joe, laughing. "I'd like one of those cube things myself!"

The three aliens laughed. "I'm afraid not. We'll have to get you back to your home planet soon, or your parents will start to worry. Hopefully you can come and see us again one day?"

Joe nodded enthusiastically as he finished his meal and walked over to the cube machine. "I'm definitely coming back for this!" He picked up a bright purple cube from the kitchen surface and looked at it in wonder.

"You can keep that one," said Isron, smiling. "Now, we'd better get back to our spaceship."

Joe pocketed the cube and exited the large metal structure with his brothers and the aliens. He was just about to start walking to the spaceship he could see in the distance when the three hoverboats came zooming up to them, leaning down so each of the brothers could climb easily inside.

"These work on land too?" asked Jack. "They're amazing!"

Joe, however, didn't look quite so convinced. "If these are the same ones as last time," he said, "I think I'd rather walk."

"Oh, this one's probably learnt his lesson," said Isron. He patted the side of the hoverboat and it jumped up and down playfully, like a dog.

It then turned to Joe, slowly hovering over to him and landing at his feet, as if apologising for what happened on the water.

Joe couldn't help but smile, and as soon as he stepped into the hoverboat, it rose into the air and zoomed over to the spaceship, with his brothers following closely behind.

Isron, Seavone and Ironson floated along beside them, keeping up with the speed of the hoverboats, something that the three brothers found very impressive indeed.

When they reached the spaceship, the three hoverboats let the boys climb out, then they zoomed off back towards the shed.

"Well, it's been wonderful showing you our world," said Isron. "Now let's get you back to yours."
Reluctantly, the three brothers agreed, and as they closed their eyes, they got beamed back onto the spaceship.

*****

Before they knew it, Tom, Jack and Joe were back in their bedroom, waking up and looking around them as if seeing their room for the first time.

Joe looked up at the skylight – day was just dawning, and the early morning light was spilling through the window, illuminating the floorboards beneath it.

"What happened?" asked Joe. "Was I dreaming?"

Tom looked over at his little brother. "Well, if you were dreaming, then so was I!"

Jack laughed. "Me too! Did we all have the same dream?"

The three brothers looked at each other, not knowing what to say or what to think.

Just then, their parents – Rosie and George – came into the room.

"What are you all doing up?" Rosie asked. "We could hear you all the way from our room!"

"You look like you've been on an adventure," added George. "But what could you have possibly got up to in this little room?"

The boys looked at each other and grinned.

"More than you'd ever think!" shouted Joe, laughing.

Rosie and George just shook their heads.

"Well, now we're all up we may as well have some breakfast," said their mum. "What do you say, boys?"

The three brothers agreed enthusiastically, jumping out of bed and following their parents downstairs to the kitchen. "I wonder if there'll be any cubes on the menu?" said Jack, making the other boys laugh as their mum and dad started making pancakes.

As the boys all sat around the table, waiting for their food, Joe announced to the room, "Well, I've decided what I want to be when I grow up."

Jack laughed. "What? An alien?"

Joe shook his head. "No, not an alien…" He paused, waiting until everyone was staring at him in anticipation. "An astronaut!"

Everyone laughed as Joe nodded to himself happily.

"Well, in order to be an astronaut," said Rosie, as she handed out the thick, fluffy pancakes, "you need a good hearty breakfast."

Joe smiled as he stuck a fork in his pancake and held it up, moving it through the air like a flying saucer.

Yes, he thought: when he was older, he'd go into space for real, and if there were any aliens out there, he'd find them.

He landed his pancake saucer on his plate, smiling, and as he put his hand into his pyjama pocket, he pulled out a small, purple cube.

The Haunted House of Mercwood

It was October, and Tom, Jack and Joe were sitting outside their little cottage in the woods with their dad, George, next to a glowing fire.

The house had been decorated for Halloween – which was the next day – and the boys were enjoying toasting marshmallows over the flames while George told them ghost stories.

"This one is actually true," he said, immediately grabbing the attention of all three of his sons. "It happened one Friday the 13th when I was about your age. It was a dark, spooky night, and me and some friends decided to go and visit Mercwood Castle."

"What's that?" asked Joe excitedly.

"It's a huge mansion (reportedly haunted) on the other side of the woods – it's still there now – and on that dark and eerie night, it looked magnificent in the pale light of the moon." George paused, looking into the distance. "It was cold, though. You could feel the cold air all around you; it gave you shivers down your back. There were owls hooting in the trees and the sky was a deep grey colour, as if thunder and lightning were on their way."

"Ooh, sounds creepy," said Jack, who was getting into the mood of the story.

"It was," replied their dad. "The castle stood dark and alone at the top of a hill, and several huge, black birds circled above it. It looked deserted – but was it?"

The three boys glanced at each other, grinning in anticipation.

"Go on!" said Tom.

"Well," responded George, "we crept inside and looked around the place, including the dark, dank dungeon. We saw some things – including the man of the house – but then the thunder and lightning started, and we ran. We ran like the wind!"

Joe leaned forward. "What do you mean, you saw some things? Who was the man of the house?"

"Ah," said George, tapping his nose with his finger. "That's for me to know, and for you to guess!"

Tom thought about this for a moment while he ate his melted marshmallow, then he looked up at his dad. "Or it's for us to find out!"

George stared at his son. "What do you mean?"

"The castle must still be there – why don't we go and see for ourselves?" Tom turned to his brothers. "It would be a great adventure, and if we go tomorrow, it'll be Halloween!"

Jack and Joe immediately agreed, but George held his hands up to stop them. "OK… but only if I come with you. I'd quite like to go in that castle again, to see if anything's changed."

Rosie – the boys' mum – came out of the cottage then, having heard everything through the window. "I'll make you all a packed lunch, and you can start off in the morning – it's quite a walk to the Castle of Mercwood."

And so it was agreed: on Halloween morning, they'd all set out for the spooky, mysterious castle.

*****

The next morning, everyone was up bright and early and Rosie waved George and the boys off as they headed to Mercwood Castle.

"It sure is chilly today," said George. "It's a good job we're all wearing lots of layers."

The three brothers agreed, not saying much as they continued on their way.

None of them would admit to it, but they were all a little nervous about what they'd find in the Castle of Mercwood. Still, their father had been before, and he was going back, so it couldn't be that bad, could it?

A few hours later, they stopped for a rest, sitting down on the cold ground and eating some sandwiches and crisps.

"How much further is it?" asked Joe, as he looked around him. The forest was so dense here that the day already seemed to be getting dark, and the walk had been longer than even George remembered it being. Soon the daylight would be gone completely.

"It really shouldn't be much further now," said their dad, as he stood up again and carried on walking. "In fact…" he jogged on for a little while and then rounded a corner in the path. "There it is!"

The brothers ran to catch up with him, all three stopping when they saw the view in front of them.

The castle was just as George had described it – old, rickety, and incredibly spooky in the half-light. It was standing on top of the hill, peering down at them, the doors and its dark windows looking like a huge, gaping face.

"Wow," said Tom, as he stared at the house.

"Are we sure we should be going in there?" asked Joe, who while still excited was now extremely nervous.

"It'll be fine," said George. "The man who lived there when I was a boy died years and years ago; it's deserted now, I'm sure of it."

With that, their dad started walking off to the house, and after only a slight hesitation, the three boys followed him.

There were hundreds of stone steps on the way up to the house, and by the time they reached the front door, all three brothers were panting, trying to catch their breath.

George, however, seemed fine, and he reached out to knock on the door. "Hello! Anyone in?"

There was silence, and Joe exchanged an anxious look with his father. "How do we get inside if there's no one here to let us in?"

George smiled as he pushed against the front door, and it creaked open slowly, the sound of the rusty hinges making the boys think it hadn't been opened for many years.

The four of them stepped inside the house, staring up in wonder at the huge entrance hall. There were two grand staircases at either side of the room, sweeping up and meeting in the middle on the floor above them. There was a huge black chandelier dangling down from the ceiling, and it was covered in cobwebs.

Actually, *everything* was covered in cobwebs – the banisters on the stairs, the lanterns next to the door, and the oil paintings hanging from the walls.

"This place looks ancient!" said Tom, coughing at all the dust around them. "Was it like this when you came?" he asked his dad.

"No," said George, shaking his head. "The lanterns and the chandelier were lit when I was here, and everything was bathed in a warm glow. Well, apart from the basement – *that* was covered in cobwebs bigger than these."

Joe shivered at the thought.

Just then, a voice boomed out around the entrance hall, deep and loud: "Who goes there?"

Joe jumped in fright, moving over to his big brothers.

George looked around him wildly. "I recognise that voice!"

"How?" asked Tom, who looked more excited than ever. "I thought you said the man you met died!"

"He did," said George, scratching his head as he wandered across the hall floor and through a door into the living room. He stopped abruptly, making his sons crash into the back of him.

"Oh," said George. "I'm sorry, we thought this place was deserted."

He was looking at the chairs in the living room, all of them old and dusty, and all of them occupied by pale, shimmery people.

"Deserted!" one of them – a large man – laughed. "Not quite."

Another of the shimmery people – a smaller boy, about half the man's age – added, "Thanks for waking up Mackruss for us; he hasn't annoyed us for days." George thought he detected a hint of sarcasm in the voice.

Tom stepped forward, looking at the people in the room with his mouth hanging open. "Are you... are you all... ghosts?"

The white, shimmery boy laughed. "We sure are! It's Halloween today, isn't it? You know it's lucky to see a ghost on Halloween!"

Tom looked round at his dad and his brothers, taking in their own pale faces. "I didn't know ghosts existed," he whispered, half scared and half amazed.

"Well, we do," said the boy ghost, as he floated over to them. "My name's Ocone. Been here centuries. Unlike Mackruss." He shook his head and rolled his eyes.

"Mackruss…" said George, staring into the distance as though he was remembering something. "Was he the man who used to live here?"

"You know him?" asked Ocone.

George nodded. "I think he was the man who lived here when I entered the house as a boy."

Ocone gasped. "I thought I recognised you! Yes, Mackruss was the man who lived here. He was evil in life and he's even more annoying in death! We've tried everything to get rid of him," he sighed, gesturing to his ghost friends, "but nothing sticks."

"Why's he so annoying?" asked Joe, who'd gotten over his fright now that he realised how friendly and normal Ocone was.

"He taunts us," said Ocone, staring at the ground. "I mean, we're ghosts too, but he haunts us! He's always making a racket, and he's always coming up with evil schemes." The ghost shuddered. "We never get a moment's peace! He's a curse on this house!"

"Oh dear," said George, staring at Ocone. "We can't have that. Isn't there a way to lift the curse?"

Ocone shook his head. "It's no good. Mackruss swore he'd stay and haunt this house forever." He paused. "Well, as long as his riddle remained unsolved."

"Riddle?" asked Jack excitedly. "We love riddles! What is it?"

Ocone sighed. "That's the trouble – we don't know. We just know that one of his relatives left it in the house for if Mackruss needed to be sorted out – his temper is well known in the family. It's written on a scroll which is kept in a box, and no ghost can open it. We've tried."

"Well, why don't we give it a go?" asked George, smiling at the ghost. "We may as well make ourselves useful while we're here!"

Ocone stared at George and his sons for a moment, looked over at his ghost friends, then floated over to the wall, vanishing straight through it.

The brothers stared at the wall in wonder, their mouths hanging open.

A moment later, Ocone appeared back through the wall, this time holding a small, ornate black and gold box.

He floated over to George and handed the box to him. "We can hold it, but our ghostly hands can't open it."

George walked over to a spare chair and sat down, looking at the box from every angle. "What do you think, boys?"

"Is there a clasp?" asked Tom.

"I can't see one," said George.

"Hmm... Open Sesame!" shouted Jack, but there was no response.

"Try and pry it open," suggested Tom, but Ocone shook his head.

"If you break it, you may not be able to get the riddle out intact," he said.

Joe took the box carefully from his father then, gave it a little shake, hearing a rattle from within. Then, after inspecting the outside, he very gently pressed down on the lid. Everyone heard a soft 'pop' sound, and then the box opened, revealing a tiny scroll.

"You did it!" shouted Ocone. "Well done! What does the scroll say?"

Even more excited now, Joe pulled out the tiny scroll, opening it to see several lines of thin, spidery writing.

"Tom, did you bring your magnifying glass?"

Tom nodded as he got the object out of his backpack – the boys were always prepared, no matter where they went or what they got up to.

Holding the scroll out to a little oil lamp that was burning in the corner of the room, Joe placed the magnifying glass over the parchment and read the words out loud:

> *"The Haunted Mercwood home*
> *Has ghosts that come and roam,*
> *But one will never leave,*
> *Will stay here to grieve.*
> *Unless you find his room,*
> *His dungeon of gloom,*
> *And say the words out loud:*
> *'Leave this ghostly crowd!'*

Be sure to sit and read,
Before you do this deed,
For if you do not,
He'll stay here to rot!"

Joe looked up at his dad. "You mentioned the dungeon before. Does it mean we have to go there?"

Ocone sighed. "If it does then we're out of luck. Mackruss had the dungeon sealed up before he died, and now there's no access door to it. Even us ghosts can't float down into it – it's as if his evil aura stops us! Oh, it's hopeless!" he shouted dramatically, throwing himself down on one of the chairs.

George smiled at him encouragingly. "Come on, Ocone, this riddle wouldn't be a riddle if there wasn't anything to solve. Now what else did it say, Joe? Something about reading?"

Joe read out loud again: "Be sure to sit and read, before you do this deed." He looked around him at the rest of the room. "Are there any books in this house?"

"Books?" asked Ocone. "Why, there's a whole library! Follow me!"

The ghost zoomed out of the room – quickly followed by his ghostly friends – and George and his sons ran to catch up. They sprinted across the entrance hall, went down a dark and dusty corridor, and then emerged into the biggest library room any of them had ever seen.

"Ta da!" Ocone looked very pleased with himself.

The boys looked around the library in wonder; there must have been at least a thousand books in there, maybe more.

"Where do we start?" asked Jack, walking over to a bookcase and pulling out a book at random.

"And what are we actually looking for?" asked Tom.

Joe looked around the room excitedly. "Don't you know anything about haunted houses? Whenever you need to get somewhere, you have to look for a secret passageway! And most of the time…"

George laughed. "It's a book on a bookcase. Good thinking, Joe."

Joe smiled, happy with his father's praise. "And I'm betting the title will be something to do with Mackruss."

"Yes!" shouted Ocone. "He's extremely obsessed with himself. Right, everyone fan out and search the books for something to do with Mackruss!"

The ghosts nodded, floating off to various corners of the room, and George and his boys started searching too.

There was silence for a good half an hour or so while they searched, and then Tom's voice rang out into the room: "What about this one? *Mackruss and the Curse of Mercwood?*"

Everyone rushed over to Tom, looking at the book and nodding in agreement.

"I hope this is it," said George. "I'm getting sick and tired of looking at books!"

"Try pulling on it," said Ocone. "But be careful!"

Very gently, Tom pulled on the book, a huge puff of dust blowing into his face as the book came loose and the bookcase creaked and rattled. A few seconds later, the entire case swung open, revealing a dark, narrow passageway.

"You've found it!" shouted Ocone. "Let's go!"

Tom hesitated. "It's a bit dark, isn't it? Shouldn't we take some lanterns or something?"

"Who needs lanterns when you have ghosts?" shouted Ocone in a singsong voice, and with that, he and his friends swooped into the passageway, their shimmery forms lighting up the narrow corridor around them.

"Wow!" said Joe, impressed. "Ghost lights are very effective!"

The boys laughed as they followed the ghosts, George bringing up the rear, and after quite a few minutes of walking – going steadily downwards the whole time – they came to a large oak door.

"This is the original dungeon door!" shouted Ocone.

"Yes, I remember it," said George, shivering slightly. As a boy, he hadn't liked the dungeon one bit.

"This must be where Mackruss hides out when he's not haunting us," said Ocone. "Remember, we need to go in there and say the line from the riddle. If we do it all together, we might have enough power to get rid of him!"

Everyone nodded, and after taking several deep breaths, they opened the door and entered the dungeon.

It was very dark, dank and damp – just as George remembered it.

As Ocone took a step forwards, a rat ran over the floor, actually going through the ghost and making him scream. This made the three brothers laugh – a ghost scared of a rat!

"Who goes there?" boomed the voice of Mackruss; it sounded like it was coming from all around them.

"It's me," said Ocone. "And I've brought some friends."

Mackruss appeared in front of them then, an old yet strong-looking ghost with black hair and even blacker eyes. He glanced at George. "I remember you – didn't I run you out of this house while I was still alive?" He laughed evilly.

"Yes," said George. "And now I'm going to do the same to you! Haunting your fellow ghosts is a ghastly thing to do, and you're not going to do it any longer!"

He glanced at his sons and his new ghost friends, nodded, then they shouted altogether: "Leave this ghostly crowd!"

"What?" asked Mackruss, staring at them in horror.

"Again!" shouted Ocone, and the group shouted once more:

"Leave this ghostly crowd!"

"But I'm the one in charge here!" shouted Mackruss, his voice quieter now.

"Leave this ghostly crowd!" they shouted again, this time at the tops of their lungs.

Mackruss started rising into the air then, looking down at the humans and the ghosts as he went. "Wait! You can't! How dare you!"

He reached the ceiling of the dungeon, looked around him, said, "Oh dear," and then vanished.

He was gone.

The curse of Mercwood Castle was solved, the haunting ghost gone.

"Oh jolly good," said Ocone, and everyone burst out laughing.

*****

George and the boys ran out of the Castle of Mercwood, laughing as they jumped down the stone steps and sprinted through the large, rusted gate.

When they were several feet into the woods, they stopped, leaning over and catching their breath.

"It's getting light," said Tom, looking up at the sky. "Were we in there all night?"

George squinted at the horizon, where the sun was rising. "Looks like it! Time seems to move differently in that house." He shrugged. "At least we won't have to walk home in the dark!"

The four of them stood for a moment, looking back at the Castle of Mercwood. Even in the morning light, the building seemed to loom over them, and Tom thought he saw a few bats fly past one of the turrets.

At least now they knew that its evil tormentor was gone, and Ocone and his friends could live there happily ever after.

"Come on, boys," said George. "Let's go home."

They all nodded, following their father into the woods.

*****

By the time the three boys and their dad arrived back at their house, they were exhausted.

Rosie came running out of the cottage as soon as she saw them. "Hello! Did you get up to anything spooky?"

"You could say that," said George, as they all walked towards the front door. "Although it's probably going to be a while before I want to even look at another book again!"

His sons laughed while Rosie raised her eyebrows.

There was a pumpkin either side of the front porch, the orange light from within them spilling out of their spiky features.

"Did you see any ghosts?" she asked, smiling to herself.

Tom, Jack and Joe looked at each other, grinning.

"Well," said Tom. "That's for us to know, and for you to guess!"

They all laughed as they entered the cottage, closing the door against the darkness of the woods.

The Land of the Lost Children

It was a lovely summer day, and in the clearing where Tom, Jack and Joe lived, the sun was shining, the birds were tweeting and everything was calm.

The three brothers were sitting on a set of swings just outside the front of their cottage, and as they gazed into the surrounding woods, they heard a creaking sound coming from behind them.

The door of the cottage opened, and their parents – George and Rosie – came through and sat on the step, looking over at their sons.

"Anything interesting happening today?" asked their father.

"Nothing at all!" cried Joe dramatically. "I'm so bored."

"Me too," agreed Tom. "We've got no idea what to do with ourselves."

Jack looked over at their parents. "Do you have any ideas? Or any stories you could tell us? If there aren't any adventures to go on, we could at least hear about some."

Rosie thought for a moment before nodding and saying, "Yes, actually, there is. I'm going to tell you a story."

"Is it an adventure story?" asked Joe, suddenly excited.

"Yes, but it's sad too," she replied, before starting the tale. "I remember when I was a girl, people around here talked of a man called Sedrick. He was a teacher at the local school and everyone loved him. I actually had him as one of my teachers at one point, and I really liked him too. But one day…" she drifted off, staring into the distance.

"What?" asked Joe, looking at his parents. "One day what?"

George chuckled. "Have some patience, Joe! She'll tell you when she's ready."

Rosie looked back at her sons and smiled. "Well, one day he took some of the children from his class on a field trip to an island. The island had a lot of myths and legends surrounding it and he was taking the children there to map out the island, and to learn all kinds of skills. But by the end of the day they hadn't returned, nor by the end of the next day, nor the next. They never came back."

"Wow," said Tom. "They're still there? What happened?"

Rosie shrugged. "Everyone believed that Sedrick must have kidnapped them, even though he was well loved around here. They said he must be evil, and that he took the kids to Misty Island with no intention of ever coming back. You see, Sedrick had no family of his own, and everyone knew that he really wanted his own children. So they thought he'd taken them there to be one big happy family."

"But what about their parents?"

Rosie sighed. "It's awful, isn't it? Many have gone to the island to try and get them back, but they always return empty handed."

"So, this 'Misty Island'," said Tom, "what are the myths and legends surrounding it?"

George spoke up then. "Well, it's said that a long time ago, fairies inhabited the island, and that's why humans don't get on very well when they visit it. They either get lost or don't find anything and leave. It's called Misty Island because of the vast mist that always seems to be there, a thick fog that people find it hard to look through. This is why they lose their way and have to give up their attempts to search any further. The people around here believe that Sedrick took the children there because he knew they'd never be able to find their way back to the shore."

The boys thought about this for a moment, and then Joe piped up, "So everyone thinks Sedrick's evil? Even though they all loved him before?"

Rosie nodded. "Once one person starts thinking along those lines, everyone else follows. Personally, I don't think we should judge anyone until we know all the facts."

Jack stood up from his swing and walked over to his parents. "I think we should go to the island and find the children!"

Rosie laughed. "Well, for one thing, they wouldn't be children any more – they'd be my age – and for another thing, it's far too dangerous! You'll get lost in the mist."

George nodded, thinking. "It's a shame. You'd think there'd be some way of getting through the mist... if only we were fairies!"

Tom and Jack leapt from their swings then and came rushing over excitedly.

"So you think fairies can walk around the island without getting lost in the mist?" asked Jack.

Rosie laughed. "In theory, yes. But of course, there's no proof that fairies actually exist."

The three brothers glanced at each other, all thinking the same thing.

"Yes there is," said Tom. "We've seen them, and we know where they live in the woods. They gave us magical water... I wonder if they have anything else we could use to go to the island."

Rosie and George stared at the boys, their mouths hanging open.

"Well," said George after a while. "After our encounter at the haunted house of Mercwood, I'll believe anything. Maybe we should pay these fairies a visit?"

Rosie nodded. "I suppose it's worth a shot if it could help find those missing people. George, you go with them. I'll get some food to put in your rucksacks."

And so it was decided.

Rosie sorted out some food and other supplies for them, and soon all three brothers and their dad were heading out into the woods. After floating down the river in canoes and walking into the trees, Tom got to a certain point and stopped.

"There's the hole we went down before. I wonder if they're all down there now or if they're out in the woods?" He looked up just in time to see some creatures in the trees, darting out of sight. They emitted a pale yellow light, and the brothers immediately knew they were fairies.

"Wait!" shouted Joe. "We need your help, please!"

There was some more movement in the trees, then Jack added, "It's about Misty Island!"

The movement suddenly stopped, and after a few seconds, one of the fairies – a small, pointy-featured creature with white wings – flew down to them, landing in front of the boys and George.

"Misty Island, you said?"

"Yes," replied Jack. "We want to go there to discover the mystery of the lost children, but we don't want to get lost ourselves."

The fairy hovered in the air for a moment, fluttering his wings as he became lost in thought.

"Is it true that the island used to be home to fairies?" George asked, who had now got over his initial shock at seeing the creature.

"Yes, that's right," said the fairy, staring into the distance. "Fairies can come and go as they please, but if a human tries to visit the island, it becomes very difficult."

"Because of the mist?" asked Joe.

"Yes, the fog," said the fairy. "We can see through it, but to human eyes it is like a thick blanket hanging in the air."

"You can see through it?" asked Jack excitedly. "Why don't you come with us, then? You can show us the way through the fog and we can try and find Sedrick and the others!"

The fairy shook his head. "I'd like to help you, but none of the fairies can be spared for the next few weeks – this time of year is very busy for us. Around the summer solstice we have a lot of work to do in the woods, keeping all the trees and plants healthy."

George chuckled. "I say, I didn't know fairies did so much!"

The fairy nodded. "It's true, so I'm afraid we can't go with you." He paused, thinking for a moment. "But I might be able to give you something that could help. Wait here."

With that, the fairy flew off in the direction of the hole in the ground, disappearing down it and appearing again just moments later with a large sack that was almost as big as he was.

He hovered over to George and the boys and handed the sack to Tom. "In here are four lanterns, but they're not just *any* lanterns – they're *magical fairy* lanterns."

Tom peered into the sack at the lights, which were already emitting the same pale yellow glow as the fairy in front of them. "Thank you, but we already have torches. We don't go anywhere without them."

The fairy shook his head. "Torches will not help you if you get lost in the fog, but these will. They're made with our very own magic, and they'll shine through the fog and guide you on your way."

"Wow!" said Joe, while the others stared at the sack in amazement.

"Plus, you should know that the fog has many mystical qualities. For one thing, time moves differently in the fog – it's as if everything stays the same, as if there is no time."

The boys didn't really understand this, but they nodded along anyway.

"The main thing you need to know is that as long as you're each holding one of these, you'll never get lost on that island, I promise you."

The boys all grinned with excitement, and George chuckled again as he held out his hand to the fairy. "Well, isn't that wonderful! Thank you very much."

The fairy looked at George's hand as if unsure what he was supposed to do, but after a while he reached out and took it, shaking it briefly before pulling his own hand back. "You're welcome. We wouldn't trust just anyone with these lanterns, but we know you're good sorts – you've asked for help before in order to heal an animal, and now you want help to save others." He smiled as he hovered in the air yet again. "Good luck on your quest! Let us know how you get on."

The four of them agreed, smiling at the fairy as he leapt into the air and flew over to a tree branch.

George looked up at the sun, which was just overhead. "If we want to get there today, we'd better get going now. Is everyone ready?"

Tom, Jack and Joe nodded at their dad. They were more than ready.

*****

A few hours later, the four of them were on the open sea, in a little boat they'd borrowed from their friend, Harry, and his mum. They'd been going for a while, and they were hoping they'd get to the island without any problems – last time they'd been on this boat, they'd got caught up in a terrible storm.

That time, they'd been searching for diamonds. This time, they were searching for people.

After another half an hour or so, Tom squinted into the distance, holding his hand up to his forehead so he could see better in the sun's glare. "Is that it?" he asked, pointing excitedly at a piece of land that was just appearing on the horizon.

George peered at the land as well. "I think so!" he shouted over the sound of the engine. "I can just about see the fog, look!"

The brothers looked, and sure enough, they could see a thick mist hovering over the island. It was thicker than any of them had imagined, and they each silently thanked the fairy for giving them the lanterns – they'd definitely be needing them.

George steered the boat towards the island, and as they were pulling up to the shore, the mist immediately enveloped them.

"Where's the sack?" cried Jack. "I can't see anything!"

"It's here!" replied Joe, opening the top. The light from the lanterns – which in the woods had been a pale yellow glow – was now a brilliant white beam, cutting through the fog and letting them see straight through it.

"It's strange," said Tom. "It's like I can see the fog, but it's also like it isn't there at all."

"Yes," agreed George. "How extraordinary! Now, help me moor the boat and then we can get out and explore."

The boys helped their father, and once the boat was secure, they each grabbed a lantern and set out onto the beach. They noticed a big boat moored further along the shore, tied to a tree.

"I wonder if that belonged to Sedrick?" asked Tom.

"It's possible," said George. "Whoever it belongs to, they didn't come back for it."

They walked from the beach over some rocks and then out onto some open land. There were a few trees dotted about here and there, but apart from that it was barren and empty.

"This is a little creepy," admitted Joe.

"It's fine!" said Tom reassuringly. "Although I can imagine it's very hard to know where you are if you haven't got these lanterns. There are no landmarks or anything to map out the island with... you'd just be going round in circles!"

"Exactly," said George, looking out over the land. "It would explain why the children never came back. As for Sedrick... we still don't know his part in this, so be careful."

The boys nodded as they continued through the fog, moving slowly so they wouldn't miss anything.

At one point, Jack looked down at his watch to see that it had stopped.

"Well, you heard what the fairy said," piped up Joe. "Time stops in the fog." The others looked at their watches too – none of them were working any more.

"Well, we'd better hurry up," suggested George. "If we have no idea what time it is, we might not get back before it starts getting dark, and I don't want to be on the ocean at night."

His sons agreed with him, and together they picked up their pace, wandering along the island.

George kept looking at his compass to make sure they were going in a straight line, and after an hour or so (at least, they thought it was an hour or so), they started to hear voices up ahead.

They sped up, George shouting out, "Who goes there?" as they ran towards the noises.

The voices suddenly stopped, but as they got closer, George and the three brothers started to make out some figures in the fog. There were about fifteen of them altogether, and one of them was much, much taller than the rest.

"Oh!" shouted the tallest figure. "People! And light! I can see through the fog! What's going on?"

The four of them rushed over to the group, and it soon became apparent that it consisted of one man and fourteen children.

"Are you Sedrick?" asked George.

The man jumped, clearly shocked. "How do you know my name? And where did you get those lights? What's going on here?"

"Don't worry," said Tom, as he took a step towards them. "We've come to rescue the children." He looked at them, amazed. They should have been his parents' age by now, but they were closer to his own age. "Wow, I guess time really does stop in the fog!"

"What do you mean?" asked Sedrick. "We've been lost for days! I never thought we'd get out of here. I've felt so bad, leading these children around, not knowing where I'm going or in which direction. I have a horrible feeling we've been walking around in circles for hours."

The three brothers looked up at their dad, who took a step closer to Sedrick and put a comforting hand on his shoulder. "I'm afraid it hasn't just been hours or days that you've been in this fog, it's been years. At least twenty. Or that's how many have passed by outside this fog, anyway."

Sedrick stared at George, his mouth hanging open. "That can't be... but... I recognise you... how do I know you?"

"You used to teach my wife, Rosie. Her last name was Knight back then. I was friends with her when she was younger too."

Sedrick took a deep breath. "But Rosie Knight is ten years old. She couldn't possibly be married!"

"I'm afraid it's true," said George, looking at the children surrounding Sedrick. They all looked incredibly scared, and he didn't blame them.

"Let's get you out of this fog," said Tom, gesturing at his lantern. "We've got a boat, and we saw another one on the beach – we assumed it was yours. We can be back on the mainland within a few hours."

Sedrick started crying then – tears of joy – and the group followed the boys and their dad out of the fog and back to the shore. They helped the teacher and the children get in the boats, and were amazed when the engines started without any problems.

"It's a miracle!" shouted Sedrick, staring back at the fog as they headed out into the open waters. "I never thought I'd leave that fog. Thank you so much!"

The boys smiled at him while Tom replied, "You should thank the magical creatures in the wood, not us!"

Sedrick stared at Tom like he was speaking gobbledygook, but then looked back out at the sea.

He just was so happy!

*****

Several hours later, they'd all got back to the mainland and George had run and called all the parents of the children from a nearby house. The parents were much older now, but when they turned up and saw their sons and daughters, they rushed over and hugged them like nothing had changed.

Sedrick stood watching the whole thing, looking nervous. "People blame me, don't they? I swear, I knew nothing about the fog when I took the children there! I just thought it sounded like a beautiful island, that I'd be able to show them things they hadn't seen before, teach them things about nature." He sighed. "I suppose they're right to blame me. I wanted a family of my own so much that I took the school kids away to a place that wasn't safe. I wasn't trying to hurt anyone!"

"No, they're not blaming you," said George. "It was the fog that kept the children there, not you. And don't worry; I'll make sure everyone knows that. But for now, you'd better get home. I imagine you'll be needing a nice hot shower and a big meal after everything you've been through!"

Sedrick sighed. "I suppose you're right; I'd better get home." He looked incredibly gloomy at the thought.

Just then, Joe piped up. "Dad, can't Sedrick come back with us for a day or two? I don't think he should be alone, and we have more than enough food and space. I'm sure Mum would like to see him too."

George smiled at his son – he was always thinking of others – before turning to Sedrick. "I think that's a wonderful idea. What do you say, Sedrick?"

The school teacher grinned widely at the thought of spending time with such a nice family. "That would be ever so kind, thank you."

"No problem!" replied George. "We may have to take a detour on the way home, though; there are some fairies we need to give something back to."

Sedrick stopped mid-stride. "Fairies?" he asked, surprised. "Gosh, the world really has changed in the last twenty years!"

Laughing, George and the boys headed off to the woods and the little cabin they called home, with Sedrick trailing happily behind them.

The Disappearance in Rennilton Woods

It was a cold, rainy day, but that didn't stop Tom, Jack and Joe from going for a nice walk in the woods – they went out whatever the weather. This time, however, their walk was a little different: they had a friend with them.

Sedrick had been enjoying the company of the boys' parents – Rosie and George – since he'd been staying with them, and he'd offered to come along for the walk should they get into any trouble. To be honest, he'd spent so long being lost on that island that the thought of a walk in the woods – no matter the weather – seemed wonderful to him.

Decked out in big coats, scarves, and gloves, they set out from their cottage in the middle of the forest, laughing and joking as they went along their way. As usual, they all had backpacks with them, filled with food, drink, and any equipment they thought they might need on their adventure.

"I like being out in the rain," said Joe happily, opening his mouth to catch some of the raindrops. "It means we get the woods to ourselves."

It was true: the weather seemed to be driving a lot of people away. Where there would usually be dog walkers and people going to and from town, they passed no one on their journey, not a single soul.

Which is why it came as such a shock when they heard something in the distance – a high pitched wailing sound, like someone was crying.

"What's that?" asked Tom, stopping in his tracks.

"It sounds like there is someone out here!" replied Jack, walking forward a few paces and straining his ears to try and listen – it was difficult to hear anything over the wind and the rain.

"Come on!" said Joe, who'd already started running ahead. "It might be someone who needs our help!"

His two brothers and Sedrick followed him, running along the path and trying not to slip on the wet stones beneath their feet. It was a little hard going, but they wanted to get to the bottom of that crying sound.

Eventually they got to a bend in the path, and walking around, they saw a girl sitting on a rock in front of them. She had her head down and she was weeping.

"Are you OK?" asked Joe, running up to the rock.

The words startled the girl, and upon seeing the three brothers and the man, she nearly fell right off the huge boulder she was sitting on. "Who are you?" she asked, still sniffling.

"I'm Joe," said the youngest of the brothers. "And this is Tom and Jack. They're my older siblings." He rolled his eyes when he said this, making the girl on the rock laugh just a little. "This here is Sedrick. He's staying with our parents for a while until he gets back on his feet."

"I'm Wendy," she replied, wiping the remaining tears from her eyes as she smiled shyly at the four of them.

"What's wrong, Wendy?" asked Jack, getting straight to the point. "We heard you crying, and we'd like to help if we can."

Wendy nodded at him. "That's very nice, but I'm not sure you can help. You see, it's my Labrador. I was walking him in the woods when something startled him and he ran away. I can't find him anywhere and I've looked all around here. He's gone, lost forever."

Tom stepped forwards, smiling encouragingly at Wendy. "Don't worry, we'll help you find him; we happen to be pretty good at finding things, don't we boys?"

Jack and Joe nodded enthusiastically.

"We've found treasure and everything," Joe replied. "I'm sure we can help find your dog."

Sedrick laughed. "Yes, and they found me, which is the most amazing thing of all. Let's get searching for your Labrador, miss. What's his name?"

"His name's Sammy; he's a chocolate lab. He's only young – he must be so frightened."

"We'll find him," said Sedrick reassuringly. "Which direction did he run off in?"

"That way," said Wendy, pointing up the path.

"Let's go!" said Joe, excited that they had a mission to complete. He liked missions.

So, the five of them – Sedrick, Wendy, Tom, Jack and Joe – continued through the Rennilton Woods, keeping their eyes peeled for any signs of a dog and shouting out "Sammy!" every so often.

So far, they hadn't found anything – not even a paw print on the ground.

The rain was easing a little by now, but it was still cold and blustery, and Joe offered Wendy his scarf to keep her neck warm. She gratefully accepted it.

They went on like this for a while, but there was no sign of Sammy, or of anyone else. It was as if the woods were completely deserted. The thought made Wendy shudder.

Looking over at Wendy, Joe noticed how sad she looked; she was no longer glancing out at the trees on either side of the path but was instead staring at her feet as she walked, letting the tears trickle down her cheeks in silence.

"Wendy, we'll find him," said Joe.

"No, we won't," she replied miserably. "The woods are too big; it's no use!"

"Don't say that," said Tom, trying to keep her spirits up. "We just need to carry on looking."

"Yeah," agreed Joe. "We have to think positively; after all, we haven't failed any of the adventures we've been on before."

Sedrick nodded. "These boys know their stuff, Wendy. Believe me."

Eventually, Wendy nodded. "OK, I believe you."

With that, the group carried on, calling out for Sammy and investigating every rustle of every bush, every animal sound coming from the undergrowth, every track on the muddy path.

After walking for what felt like hours, Sedrick came to a stop. "Wait."

"What is it?" asked Jack, suddenly on the alert.

Sedrick took a few steps further along the path, holding his hand out to stop the boys and Wendy from following him. "I think I can see something... good grief!" he shouted, before turning round to face the others. "There's a clearing over there, and it's filled with animal cages!"

"Cages?" asked Joe, standing on his tiptoes to try and see what Sedrick was talking about.

"Cages with animals in them," said Sedrick, quietly now. "Those are poachers."

"Poachers?" gasped Wendy. "Do you think they have Sammy?"

"I don't know," replied Sedrick, "but what I do know is that we have to investigate. If we can save those animals, if we can run the poachers out of these woods..."

"Yes!" said Joe, his heart thumping with excitement. "We can't let them get away with this!"

"Listen to me," said Sedrick, "we need to be careful. The poachers could be dangerous."

The boys nodded in agreement, but before they could stop her, Wendy ran off ahead of them, desperate to get her dog back. "You can't do this!" she yelled as she ran towards the cages in the clearing. "You can't keep these poor animals locked up; it's not right!"

Jack and Joe ran after her, but when Tom tried to follow, Sedrick grabbed hold of his sleeve, pulling him back. "Shh, let's hide behind these ferns," he whispered. "If we all get caught by the poachers, there's nothing we can do."

Tom wanted to run after his brothers, but he knew that Sedrick was right, so he remained quiet as he watched from behind the ferns.

He saw Wendy standing amongst the animal cages, looking around wildly at the various creatures that had been caught, then he watched as Jack and Joe caught up to her.

While they were searching for Sammy, two big, burly men crept up behind them, taking them by surprise.

"Looks like we'll need those extra cages after all, Sumie," said one of the men, laughing at Wendy, Jack and Joe.

"You're right, Zacron," said Sumie. "Help me get them into the cages."

"We've only got two spare," said Zacron. "What shall we do?"

"Put the boys in them. The girl won't run off, not while we've got her friends," replied Sumie.

As Jack and Joe were being locked up in the cages, Tom and Sedrick quietly ran in the other direction.

"We need to find help," said Sedrick. "I know where the forest warden's hut is – it's not far. Let's go, quickly!"

With that, they ran off into the woods, away from the direction of the poachers.

It didn't take them long to get to the forest warden's hut, and as they got there, a man and a woman came out of it.

"John!" said Sedrick, looking at the man in the green warden outfit. "I'm afraid we've got into a bit of trouble with some poachers over in the big clearing. Tom's brothers have been captured, as well as a girl called Wendy."

"Wendy!" shouted the woman, who Sedrick now saw had tears running down her cheeks. "That's my daughter – I'm out here looking for her. She took the dog for a walk hours ago and didn't come back."

"We were helping her look for her dog," explained Sedrick. "He ran off into the woods. I'm so sorry, but she ran off towards the poachers before I could stop her."

"Oh, it's not your fault," the woman replied, placing a hand on Sedrick's arm. "Wendy's always running off on her own and getting into trouble! At least I know where she is now. Will you help me to get her back?"

Sedrick nodded, and so did John. "Of course."

"I'm Sophie, by the way," said the woman, smiling a little now.

"I'm Sedrick, and this is Tom."

"Right," said John. "Let's go and sort these poachers out!"

*****

Meanwhile, back in the clearing, Jack and Joe were trying to get out of their cages, but it was no good – the poachers had taken their backpacks off them, and they had nothing they could try and pick the lock on the cages with. They needed something sharp, or something they could slide into the lock.

Wendy, on the other hand, had a different kind of approach. She thought that if she was nice to the poachers, she would be able to get them on her side.

"Why do you poach animals?" she asked innocently.

"Stop talking!" said Sumie. "You're giving me a headache."

Wendy glanced at Jack and Joe – so much for her plan.

"I'm going to go and get some firewood, boss," said Zacron. "Will you be OK here?"

"I'll be fine," grumbled Sumie. "I can handle a few kids."

Zacron left, and once he was out of sight, Sumie walked to the other side of the clearing and sat down on a blanket that had been placed on the ground. He looked exhausted after a full day's poaching.

Wendy had by now spotted Sammy, her chocolate Labrador, in one of the cages. She was standing next to it and stroking his fur through the bars, trying to comfort him. "Don't worry, Sammy. We'll get you out of here," she whispered.

Joe was shaking the bars of his cage, trying to get Sumie's attention, but Wendy shushed him.

"He might fall asleep," she whispered.

And that – after a few minutes – is exactly what Sumie did.

With Zacron still gone, Wendy crept over to the sleeping poacher and very carefully lifted his set of keys out of his pocket.

Creeping back over to the boys, she tried to find the right key to Joe's cage.

"Come on," said Joe, "before the other one gets back!"

"Shh!" said Wendy. "He might hear you and wake up!"

Eventually, Wendy found the right key, and sliding it into the lock, she turned it until she heard a click.

The door of the cage opened with much more force than she'd expected, and Joe – who had been pressing against it in his eagerness to get out – went flying into the dirt in the clearing.

"Blimey, you were in a hurry," whispered Wendy, trying not to laugh at the sight of Joe sprawled out on the ground.

Jack was laughing quietly to himself in his own cage, and Wendy let him out with another one of the keys.

"You OK, Joe?" Jack asked, still chuckling as his brother stood up and brushed himself off.

"Yeah," he replied, a little embarrassed at having fallen over in front of Wendy. "Come on, let's hurry before Zacron comes back."

Wendy froze on the spot. "I can hear whistling, I think he's coming back now!"

A moment later, the second poacher appeared in the middle of the clearing. He looked at Sumie asleep on the blanket and then at the Jack, Joe and Wendy. "Hey! Where do you kids think you're going?" he asked.

Still frozen to the spot, Wendy screamed as Zacron ran over to her and grabbed her arm.

She instinctively trod on his foot, making him shout out, and while he was distracted, Joe jumped on Zacron's back. With Jack and Wendy's help, they pushed him into the cage Joe had just been in, slamming the door and locking it as quickly as they could.

By now, Sumie had woken up, and when he ran over to the three of them, they did the exact same thing to him: they jumped on his back, pushed him into the remaining spare cage, and locked him in there.

"That's where you two belong!" shouted Jack triumphantly, pleased at how well their little mission had gone.

With that, he turned and high fived Joe and Wendy. "I think we make a very good team."

"I think so too," said Wendy. "And thank you for helping me find Sammy." With that, she walked over to the cage her dog was in, unlocking it and letting him out.

He was so happy to be out of the cage that he jumped up at her, licking her face and wagging his tail. He then thanked Joe and Jack in the same way.

Just then, John, Sedrick, Tom and Sophie appeared in the clearing.

"We've come to rescue you!" said Sedrick. "But I see you didn't actually need our help!" He was laughing, amazed at how the boys had got out of the cages, replacing themselves with the poachers.

Sophie ran over to her daughter, leaning down and bringing her in for a big hug. "Oh, Wendy, I was so worried!" she shouted, before realising Sammy was there too. "And you found him! Oh, well done!"

Sammy jumped up at Sophie, licking her face as well. He was just so happy to see everyone.

John the forest warden walked over to the cages that held Sumie and Zacron. "Well, well, what have we got here? We've been looking for you for months! How dare you come into Rennilton Woods and poach our animals! Shame on you."

Sumie and Zacron had the good grace to look ashamed, though the brothers were sure this was an act.

"And how dare you treat my daughter in this way!" shouted Sophie, walking over to the cages as well. "You'll be going away for a long time, and good riddance!"

John spoke into his walkie talkie then, asking for the police to come to the big clearing in Rennilton Woods. "They'll soon be where they belong," he added.

"Right!" said Sedrick to Tom, Jack and Joe, "we'd better get you boys back home!"

"Are you their father?" asked Sophie.

"Oh no," replied Sedrick. "Their parents have been kind enough to let me stay with them for a while, but it's time I moved on." He paused, laughing. "I'm just not sure where to move on to."

Wendy's mum thought for a moment. "Well, we have a guest house at the end of our cottage. You could stay in it, if you like. As a thank you for helping Wendy today."

Sedrick smiled, patting Sammy the Labrador on the head as he considered the offer. "That sounds lovely, thank you!"

"You should come and have a look at it now," said Wendy, suddenly excited. "You can help chop the firewood for us – it's a hard thing to do when there's no man of the house around."

Sophie blushed at that. "Yes, please come for dinner. You can have a look at the guest house. We'd love to have you."

Sedrick accepted the offer gratefully. "Boys," he said, turning to Tom, Jack and Joe. "Please tell your parents that

I'll be back later. Right now, I have a guest house to look at!"

The brothers laughed, pleased at how happy Sedrick seemed to be.

"OK, but only if we're allowed to come and visit," said Tom.

"Yes!" shouted Wendy happily. "Come whenever you like."

With that, everyone said their goodbyes, and while John waited in the clearing for the police to arrive, Sedrick, Wendy, Sophie and Sammy left together. They already looked like a happy little family.

Tom, Jack and Joe started walking off in the opposite direction, back towards their home.

"I'm glad Sedrick's found a family of his own," said Joe. "He's seemed a little lost since he got back from that island."

"Well, he's not as lost as he was when he was on the island," pointed out Jack, making his brothers laugh.

"I'm sure he'll be happy living at Wendy and Sophie's house," said Tom. "And we can still visit."

As they continued through the Rennilton Woods towards their cottage, they could smell their mum's cooking wafting along the path. It smelled delicious.

"Ah, home sweet home," said Joe excitedly.

"Yes," agreed Jack. "It's much better than cage sweet cage. I couldn't have stayed locked in there much longer!"

Tom laughed. "I don't know how we get ourselves into these situations, but I'm glad we always get out of them again."

"Yes," replied Joe, "through some good old teamwork."

He turned to high five his brothers, and they high fived him back, laughing the whole time.

It had been another great adventure.

9 781784 655648